Relative *to* Wind

ALSO BY PHOEBE WANG

Waking Occupations
Admission Requirements

Relative *to* Wind

ON SAILING, CRAFT, AND COMMUNITY

PHOEBE WANG

Assembly Press

PRINCE EDWARD COUNTY, ONTARIO

Library and Archives Canada Cataloguing in Publication

Title: Relative to wind : on sailing, craft, and community / Phoebe Wang.
Names: Wang, Phoebe, author
Identifiers: Canadiana (print) 20240419162 | Canadiana (ebook) 20240419170 | ISBN 9781738009824 (softcover) | ISBN 9781738009831 (EPUB)
Subjects: LCSH: Sailing. | LCGFT: Essays.
Classification: LCC GV811 .W36 2024 | DDC 797.124—dc23

Published by Assembly Press | assemblypress.ca
Cover and interior designed by Greg Tabor
Edited by Andrew Faulkner

Printed and bound in Canada on acid-free 100% post-consumer recycled fibres in line with our commitment to ethical business practices and sustainability.

Table of Contents

Boat Words

A ROPE ON A BOAT is never a rope—it's a line, sheet, or halyard. The boat doesn't turn left or right but to port or starboard. If you're walking to the front of any watercraft, you're going forward to the bow. When you're moving toward its rear, you're moving aft to the stern.

You could draw a boat and label it, but why do that when you can pick up boat words the way a child might? By pointing up at the spreaders, the spars that act like crosstrees extending from the mast. By curling your fingers around the shrouds, the boat's wire rigging. By remembering that the lifelines are the vinyl-coated wires around the perimeter of the boat when you grab onto them to steady yourself. By pestering the skipper with questions—*What's this? What's that?* Your eagerness earns you a spell on the tiller, and you feel the weight of the water streaming against the rudder. Trip over one of the hard, small parts on the boat and land on your knees, swearing and embarrassed at everyone's quick concern. You'll remember the cleat, block, or winch like the name of someone you instantly dislike. Not knowing these names is as clear a sign of a landlubber as wearing sneakers that leave skid marks on the deck. Not knowing means you'll be corrected until you do.

Someone will ask you to lug a jib sail in its heavy, awkward bag from below. Sails are no longer made of cotton or linen canvas but of a polyester fibre known as Dacron. Spread out like wings against a greyish-pink sky, their plasticky edges are taut with purpose, curving against the wind. The big triangle sail along the mast is the main. It's printed with a unique number, assigned by the boat builder or sailing association. The sail at the front of the boat is the foresail or headsail, either a genoa or jib, depending on its cut. A genoa, affectionately called the genny, extends beyond the mast and is used for lighter to moderate winds, as it has a larger surface area, while a jib sail is smaller and used for higher winds. There's also the spinnaker, which is made of thinner nylon of plain or coloured material and resembles a parachute, giving it its nickname. "Let's fly the chute" and "Douse the chute" are common commands during a regatta when sailing downwind.

The sails might power the boat, but it's the lines and sheets that control its speed. Their names are shouted by crew during times of activity and stress, which does nothing to decrease that stress. The lines that raise each sail are referred to as halyards—when they accidentally fly to the top of the mast, referred to as "skying the halyard," it's a tragicomedy. There are topping lifts, lines that hold up the boom or the whisker or spinnaker poles. Lines that attach to the bottom of a sail are known as sheets, such as the mainsheet, which goes through a device known as the mainsheet traveller and is used to decrease or increase the boat heel. Heel is the sideways angle of the boat as it leans over. Jib sheets, attached to the clew end of the sail, run along the edge of the boat through pulley blocks and around winches on the starboard and port sides of the boat. Winches look like big metal spools, and I fidget with them when they aren't being used because they make satisfying clicking sounds. Other rigging lines include the cunningham, which sounds like something dirty; the reefing line; the boom vang; and the outhaul. Are you still with me?

Your brain might be feeling overpowered by this deluge of terminology, unable to maintain its usual course through the English language. I promise that when you get under sail, these names have textures and weights that will help you remember them. Reading isn't how I, or how most sailors, learn phrases like "ready to come about" or "raise the main." We learn them when the skipper gives a brusque direction that sends us scrambling for the right line, only to have an experienced, empathetic crew member point it out. Lines are learned by their colours, plain or braided, white with woven red or blue strands. They're learned by position and feel. They're acquired through error, like when you accidently release a spinnaker halyard instead of a pole lift. They accumulate with each race, cruise, and season, attaching themselves to verbs such as hoisting, hauling, heaving to, heading up, bearing off, letting out, easing, trimming, tacking, and gybing. Knowledge of these manoeuvres and how they relate to each other develops in a layered way. It's part of the slow learning process: feeling confused when "tacking" is used to refer to a boat turning, frustrated when the explanation of "port tack" and "starboard tack" requires more terms that you don't know, and embarrassed when you forget the difference and have to be retold. Yet as your fluency and competency grow, you comprehend better the beautiful complication, or complicated beauty, of sailing.

The confusion and obfuscation caused by the language of sailing is, simultaneously, what makes sailing-speak useful for giving directions. Sailors value both specificity and efficiency, as evidenced by a command such as "Ease the jib." This short phrase can be translated as: "The wind has now shifted, as you may have observed, so grab the rope attached to the little sail—the one you were just holding while you were sheeting it in—and release it from its cleat, gently letting it out until I say stop or until you have ascertained that the sail is no longer luffing." But who has time to say all that? Optimally, the crew would notice the shifting conditions and trim the sails without having to be told, since this is more or less their only job. As satisfying as boat-speak is, there's more satisfaction in not having to say anything at all.

There was a difference in how our skipper spoke to us in our first years of racing and how he spoke when he was reviewing the race with other skippers, on land again, tall cans of Old Milwaukee in their hands. I stood shyly aside, knowing few people beyond our crew. Wind conditions and tacking decisions were discussed, praise given, regrets expressed. My attention slipped in and out of the impenetrable dialect of sailors, and I was confused by why the same story was recounted over and over again. I wouldn't know the pleasure of retelling, rehashing, and filling in gaps until many seasons later. Until I knew my job well enough that I could spare a few moments to squint across the harbour at what other crews were doing, until I had accumulated my own victories and griefs. I would hear the boat phrases come out of my mouth, self-consciously, and wait for confusion or correction.

I wanted ardently to sound like a sailor, since I didn't look or feel like one.

Nautical terminology is rooted in Old and Middle English, imported by way of Germanic and Norse roots. Its monosyllabic grippy and sticky sounds harken back to the flexible, clinker-built Viking ships that wove their way through the Baltic Sea carrying cargo or invaders. While ships have evolved, terms such as *bow* and *stern* remain unchanged. *Bow,* meaning "the forward part of a ship" that begins where the sides move inward, is derived from the Old Norse *bogr* and an earlier proto-Indo European root, *bheug-,* meaning "to bend." These terms are related to words for bent or curved objects, such as *akimbo, bight, bog,* and *bow* as a verb and as a weapon for shooting arrows. According to *The Dictionary of Nautical Literacy, bow* is derived from *bog* in Low German and Dutch, meaning "shoulder or arm," so in Middle English the "shoulders" of a boat's hull began to be known as the "bow." The etymology of *stern* is more straightforward, deriving from Old Norse *stjorn,* meaning "control" or "steering," and the Old Frisian word *stiarne,* meaning "rudder." In boat words, I can hear the creak of wood timbers, commands shouted to the crew across a vessel pitching in autumn winds, and the wind itself, knocking bodies and shoving objects about. I hear the romance of a life at sea and its accompanying perils.

Language can function as both a barrier and an entry point into an identity, and in the case of the language of sailing, it kept me out before it let me in. Its arcane impenetrability feels purposeful, like a code. This inaccessibility may be a result of its etymology and how its meanings have diverged from English words of common usage. Sailing's distinct idioms are, in large part, a result of British naval history. Sailors took pride in the stories and skills that made their profession unique from other branches of the military, and this pride is reflected in naval songs and anthems such as "Heart of Oak" and in nautical expressions. Yet from the seventeenth century into the eighteenth century, civilians—fishermen, longshoremen, and men on merchant ships, even criminals—were forcibly conscripted through impressment for military service. The harsh life on board and the brutal punishments for deserters must've felt like a continual hazing.

All of this colonial violence—conscription practices, hierarchies of rank, naval wars, and transport of raw resources—has steeped into the language like tea leaves in scalding water. These were the same seamen and ships that held enslaved peoples in cargo holds, encountered Indigenous peoples on Turtle Island, mapped coastlines, and claimed harbours for shipping ports. The English language also travelled by sea, as much an import as systems of government, laws, and policies. British ships brought opium to the ports of Hong Kong, the islands where my family lived with the sound of the waves at their doorsteps. Remnants of this history are still present in nautical terms and sayings, many of which have entered everyday English. Idioms such as "all hands on deck," "long shot," "toeing the line," "run a tight ship," and "knowing the ropes" are shadowed with the strict protocols of sailing and its militaristic, subjugating narrative. These phrases are time capsules, an archive animated by the act of sailing, which brings the past into the present.

I love to tell the story of how my parents met. They are both from Hong Kong but, being from different social classes, met after immigrating to Canada. They were tenants in the same boarding house in Toronto's Chinatown East area on Gerrard Street and quickly fell in love. Eventually, they moved to Ottawa and started a family—my younger sister and I. My first words were in Cantonese, but my parents began speaking English to me before I entered kindergarten. Even though I've spoken and written in English for most of my life, I still feel that I have a slippery grasp of the language. I became a writer to give myself more time to pin down what I really mean. Speaking in English is an ongoing negotiation of meaning and implication. My parents speak English with blunt directness, translating the syntax of Cantonese imperatives, tenses, and word order. When they use idioms, it's with slow delibera-tion. My own diction is wide but arcane, gleaned from the Victorian novels I read in my teenage years. In high school I knew what *reticule, petticoat, scoundrel,* and *sovereign* meant but I struggled with *Simpsons* references. I avoided *fuck* and *shit* and *asshole* not out of a dislike for profanity but because it felt fake whenever I swore. My self-consciousness with small talk and banter might be more to do with shyness than with my immigrant background, but the two aren't inseparable. My mother tongue, Cantonese, can feel foreign to me because while it was the first language I heard, I haven't developed a complete fluency in it. My aunties and uncles have praised my accent and ability, but that is because I have learned that speaking Cantonese, being Cantonese, requires a certain attitude, a brashness and wit, just as conversing in Canadian English requires tact and a determined friendliness. Thinking between two languages, without an unthinking fluency in either, has highlighted the performative aspect of speech.

These questions about the relationship between language,

experience, and identity are not unique to sailing. When I began teaching ESL, I absorbed the lexicon of learning outcomes and lesson plans. There's the patter of hockey announcers that I picked up while watching the Vancouver Canucks ascend through playoff rounds, full of offsides, penalties, dekes, and wraparound goals. The academic jargon of literary criticism, precisely impenetrable with its examination of liminalities, marginalities, and subversions. The shoptalk of writers when they compare publishers and contracts and mull over drafts and intentions. Sociolinguists call this kind of manoeuvrability through different registers code-switching, and I shift into these specific registers with varying degrees of consciousness. When I felt unsure about whether I identified with a role, I built my confidence through speaking the language until it no longer felt like a performance. In sailing, learning follows a different order. Knowing what a boat part or manoeuvre is called doesn't necessarily clarify its purpose. Descriptions and diagrams aren't enough—the understanding only comes through the feel of the boat turning into the wind, or the hull tilting underneath me when a gust hits.

Taking up sailing as a pastime in which I might never feel fluent may be an unconscious desire to seek comfort in discomfort. It is almost assuaging to have such a conscious sense of unbelonging. Despite this, I still find the evocation of words like *leeward* and *layline* to have a compelling charm, a spell on my spirit. It's possible that I veer away from critiquing the embodied practice of learning this diction and what it might mean as a colonized subject to take up a sport with a brutal and bloody history. It's as if I desire at least one recreation that is a literal and metaphorical escape. Maybe it's a relief to subjugate my identity into that of being a crew member, or to spend a few hours a week with my mind and senses engaged in the immediate tasks of skirting and trimming sails rather than the endless ways I'm complicit and accountable.

When I hear a land acknowledgement, or when I myself speak the names of the Indigenous peoples on whose traditional territory I reside, the words press into my heart. I'm aware that Toronto Harbour has historically moored tall ships carrying settlers and cargo. For some reason, it didn't occur to me for many seasons to reflect whose land my yacht club occupies. Queen City Yacht Club (QCYC) is located on Algonquin Island, previously known as Sunfish Island and renamed to acknowledge the Indigenous presence in the area. Land acknowledgements and names are meaningful but are only the beginning of the work of decolonization and reconciliation. Asking how sailing might be decolonized is like sailing into a hole—a word sailors use to describe a patch on open water where the wind has died. Boats caught in a hole drift aimlessly in irons until a breeze lifts them out of it. Skippers watch for these holes by sighting boats with sagging sails and avoid them by tacking around the area. But every boat inevitably stalls. While crews on tall ships making voyages across the Atlantic dreaded being becalmed, I now think it can be necessary and useful to pause mid-voyage and reflect on the costs of the journey.

Sailing evolved from a military occupation to a recreational sport in the nineteenth century, with the initiation of races such as America's Cup in 1851. When clubs were founded along the eastern seaboard in the latter half of the nineteenth century, sailing became the pastime of an upper-class, heterosexual, white, male demographic. How much of this colonial history is present in recreational racing today? Sailing is still inflected with associations of class and privilege. Images of an old-money clan cruising out of a New England port on a gleaming wooden yacht, or of a crew in matching sponsored jerseys, working mechanical winches in perfect coordination on a boat costing hundreds of thousands of dollars, contributes to the idea of sailing as exclusionary and cliquish. I've visited a club with a dress code, where white families bowled on manicured lawns while Asian wait staff mixed Bloody Marys.

However, at many yacht clubs around Lake Ontario, sailing is a much more modest pastime, though club memberships, docking fees, the cost of a boat and its maintenance, gas, and other miscellaneous add-ons lead owners to refer to boats as "holes in the water where you throw money." My image of a typical lake sailor is now a retired couple dressed in paint-splatted shorts and ball caps, or a group of guys in dirty boat shoes and wraparound reflective sunglasses. I belong to a club whose commodore, the first year I crewed, was a Japanese Canadian woman, which made me realize that sailors could look like me. Gradually, I have seen more new members who don't fit the stereotypical image of a skipper or racer. Much more can be done to improve sailing's inclusivity, but my own presence at the club is a sign of the evolution of the sport's identity and its shifting values. The language may not change, but its users have.

That identity is inflected with paradoxes—sailors are the kind of people who hope for the best but prepare for the worst. Buying a boat to fulfill a longing for smooth sailing is somewhat oxymoronic. With the time, expense, and expertise required, there's as much pain involved as pleasure. Cruisers outfit their boats until they resemble floating hardware stores and medic stations, chart courses to anchorages and moorings, and make countless other preparations for the sake of escaping for a trip of several weeks. Racers who sign themselves up for casual weeknight club races or regattas also pour in time and energy for insubstantial rewards. On the racecourse, crews will attempt to force their competitors over the line early, only to later offer spare parts to the very boat they nearly ran afoul of. It's a fine balance to have enough, but not too much, competitive spirit. Taking things too seriously—whether it's holding grudges or dwelling too long on mistakes—takes the fun out of a race and of the spirit of affectionate heckling and wry complaining. Complaining and chirping are already part of my personality, so I have no issues with those identifications. I find other contradictions in the sailors I know, who desire to be social and to be left alone at the same time. They are helpful but can be testy. They'll head to the club with every intention of finishing a messy, bothersome task on their boats, only to spend half the day puttering about and sipping something cold and carbonated. These quirks are endearing, yet I'm apprehensive to find them in myself.

Recently, I headed down to Ward's Island Beach with a non-sailing friend. I took note of the wind, steadily pushing clouds from a southwesterly direction.

"It's supposed to rain," my friend said as we boarded the QCYC club tender.

"No, I think the wind'll push the clouds over the lake," I surmised. From the beach, we watched sailboats coming through the Eastern Gap and out into the lake.

"Where are they all going?" she asked me, as they appeared heeling on the water as if pulled on a string.

"It looks like they're headed out for a cruise, maybe to Scarborough or Whitby," I said. I started to explain I could tell because their canvas dodgers were up, giving the skippers protection from the sun, and I could see the sun's glint on the BBQs mounted on their stern rails. But my friend had already laid back down on her towel, so I didn't add that they were heeling on a port tack in what looked like eight to ten knots, perfect conditions for a cruise on the lake.

After years of accumulating a very specific set of terminology that I rarely use outside the context of sailing, I realize that it's not learning words and phrases that has transformed how I see and move through the world. It's sailing in rainstorms and sauna-like summer humidity. It's sanding hulls, rigging dinghies, and steering boats under heavy gusts and light air days. Racing in Toronto Harbour and in Lake Ontario from Ashbridge's Bay to Port Credit and helming a boat to Niagara-on-the-Lake. Jumping off bows to swim with the boat anchored at Ward's Island Beach and climbing centreboards to right a capsized dinghy. Pushing Albacores and Quests while wading into lake water and casting off on bigger keelboats like J30s and Viking 33s. It's not a question of whether or not sailing has become a part of my identity, but how much, and how deeply.

For those of you still learning, like me, to use your senses and skills to reach your destination, I can promise that after the boat is put away and you're safe in port, you'll look for willing ears to pour out your trials and triumphs. You'll find yourself in possession of a unique and astounding story, a story told in its own uncommon language.

Becoming Crew

WILL I MAKE IT will I make it will I?

It's a few minutes past five on a sharp spring afternoon. I gaze ahead at the dove-grey slice of lake. It's not far, but there are so many crosswalks and intersections slowing me down. Every time a big red hand goes up, I'm forced to stop running. I suck in big breaths of air, check my phone, and wedge my body ahead of the other pedestrians. People—there are so many people in my way. Office workers power-walking to Union Station, tourists walking three or four abreast, couples arm in arm, Blue Jays fans clogging York Street near the stadium. I jog underneath the Gardiner Expressway and across streetcar tracks toward the waterfront. To anyone watching, I look like another irritable, impatient Torontonian. I feel like I'm fleeing and chasing something at the same time.

I'm going to make it. The *Algonquin Queen II* is rounding the *Sundial Folly* sculpture and pulling up at the dock. A biker dings his bell through the seagulls and club members with Sobeys bags flapping at their feet. I've made it. I fill and refill my lungs while looking out at the lake criss-crossed by island ferries. In the early part of the century, the harbour was crowded with docks, wharves, and sheds, and watercraft of all shapes and sizes—paddle steamers, passenger steamboats, lumber carriers, skiffs, and, in winter, iceboats. But today, I take in a view uncluttered by history.

Still out of breath, I join the loose hoop of members and guests waiting for Queen City Yacht Club's tender boat. The schedules aren't a secret, but since only members or their guests can book a ticket and board the tender, not many Torontonians know about these club ferries. On race nights, the tender runs every half-hour and drops off passengers right in front of the club on Algonquin Island. There are other options to reach the island, such as the city ferries or the water taxis, but they're not as convenient or as pleasant. Following an unspoken etiquette, we wait while people with bikes and grocery carts board first. Senior members flash their membership cards and board while the rest of us line up to pay with cash or tickets. The *Algonquin Queen II* has a capacity of forty-nine and I have to admit I like the feeling of exclusivity. As I slowly move down the ramp to the tender, I leave behind another Phoebe, the stressed-out, overworked Phoebe, like a shadow that cannot leave shore.

During sailing season, I hurry from tutoring centres and ESL schools and offices across the city. I bike from different apartments to arrive on time. I arrange work schedules to have Wednesday evenings at liberty, and when I can't leave students or escape a meeting early, my mind wanders to the lake, where the rest of the crew are unwrapping lines and sails. From early May to late September, sailors around Lake Ontario understand these rituals. We pack bags with Sperrys, sunglasses, lanyards, sunscreen, gloves, and snacks. We dress in layers. We text boat owners looking for extra crew. We work through lunch so we can power down our laptops at 4:00 p.m. to get over to the island and ready our boats before the race committee makes its starting signals. We don't take this for granted. Sailing season is short as a Canadian summer.

A change of state comes over me when, after a prolonged winter, I step onto the tender and feel its tilt and sway. I'm on the water now. I stand among chit-chatting crew. If I'm in a social mood, I'll ask after kids and winter vacations. But often I'm silent, watching the city retreat and squinting to see if I recognize any of the Vikings and Beneteaus heeling on the lake. I note the wind direction and the stack of clouds over Humber Bay. I estimate how many knots of wind might be fanning the tender's flag, though when the sun lowers, it'll inevitably drop off.

There are many rituals. In the weeks leading up to launching their boats, owners don workpants and old sweaters. They'll climb ladders to their boats nestled high in their cradles and peel back the covers, hoping not to find too much ice in the cockpit or to have to evict a family of rodents or birds. Rubbing their chilly hands, they'll start investigating for dampness, rot, mould, and rust, adding to the list of repairs and tasks made when the boats were hauled out of the water at the end of last season. As the ground warms and the trees start to bud, the boatyard will become vocal with hammers, sanders, and the occasional bad word. Owners depressed and flummoxed by a task can usually find a sympathetic ear, a bit of advice, a spare part, or all three. Owners who left their boats in good repair take pleasure in the brightwork and polishing and varnishing the wood trim. On launch weekends, teams of senior members push each boat cradle onto rails so they can be driven down the marine railway and launched with their owners sitting in the cockpits like minor royalty on a parade float. Eager to be in the proximity of a sailboat again, I too have done my bit of sanding and painting of keels and hulls. Though I'm not a boat owner, I'm just as impatient to see them afloat again, lined up in their moors and slips.

After a fifteen-minute crossing, the *Algonquin Queen II* draws up alongside the white-painted, two-storey clubhouse. My gaze takes in the balconies and planters of flowers. I thank the crew as I step onto the dock, make my way to the club wash-rooms for one last stop, then shortcut along the marine railway toward the south gate. I pass the bigger boats in their slips, the cottonwood trees that drop sticky yellow buds each spring. The long line of masts shifts in the breeze along Algonquin and Ward's Island, accompanied by the tinkling sound of metal snaps and stays. Boats that don't race expectantly await their owners, like unopened gifts. I pass other crews unplug-ging extension cords and unzipping sail covers. When I reach *Panache*, the 26-foot Niagara I crew on, I don't have to ask per-mission as I step over the lifelines and onto the deck.

Mark, the owner and skipper, feels my weight on the boat before his eyes crinkle in greeting. Because he is my friend and roommate, I frequently ignore and make fun of him, but because he is also my skipper and the person responsible for steering the boat and instructing the rest of us to carry out manoeuvres, I have to pay attention to him. We grin at each other in silent acknowledgement of this shift, then he contin-ues a story he was in the middle of telling to Phil or to Pat, already on board. I leap down to the cabin, stow my knapsack on the floor, put my beer in the locker, and peer up at Mark with jib sheets under my arm.

"There was a lot of breeze in the harbour," I report.

"We'll go with the number two then," Mark says, lowering the outboard motor and plugging in the fuel line. Handing the jib sheets to Phil, who starts unwrapping them, I find the right sail and haul it up onto the foredeck, or the bow of the boat, unzipping the bag to find the tack and clew ends. I clip the jib to the forestay with the snap hooks along the edge of the leech, then sit on the deck tying bowline knots on the jib sheets, which I run outside of the shrouds but inside the lifelines, through the blocks, loosely around the winches, ending with a figure-eight knot to keep the lines from sliding out. This was the first knot I learned, and I can make them without thought now.

In my first season crewing, I felt a plunging disbelief that I was able to spend time on a sailboat, and the feeling still hasn't quite left me. I didn't grow up sailing, and I believed that no one in my family had either. But my parents are islanders, and my mother tells me that my great-grand-mother lived on a houseboat in Hong Kong's Aberdeen Harbour. Like most people unfamiliar with the sport, I imagined uniformed crew outfitted in hundreds of dollars worth of Gore-Tex, moving in coordination on a huge yacht slicing through ocean waves. I imagined millionaires' playthings, Olympic athletes in bright jerseys, and lone, eccentric teenagers embarking on oceanic journeys.

I'm not old, white, or rich. I don't think I fit anyone's expectations of a sailor, as evidenced by the looks of surprise I get when I bring it up to family, friends, and fellow writers. Their assumptions exhaust me, and I don't always have the energy to explain how I began racing, how active the sport of sailing is on the Great Lakes, or the special atmosphere at Queen City. As a result, some people have known me for years and not known that I've sailed. In the mirror is a petite Asian woman with a round, serious face who looks like she spends more time in the library than doing rigorous physical activity. Peering closer, I see the bruises on my shins and my foul-weather gear hanging on hooks. But on occasion, someone corners me with their curiosity. "I hear that you sail," they say, and the words spill out of me. They ask how I started, where I sail, whether it's an expensive sport. I watch for bewilderment or eyes glazing over at the stream of boat words that I can't help using and that I try to define for them, but curiosity is a hatch I could pull someone through to a club visit or race, where they too might surprise themselves.

I tell people that QCYC is one of the oldest sailing clubs in Toronto, as comfortable and informal as a hoodie softened by the sun. There's no dress code—I sail in a uniform of old jeans and a ball cap, and my foul-weather gear consists of a $20 pair of rain pants, hand-me-down gloves of dissolving leather, and a Columbia hiking jacket. No makeup, just sunscreen and my hair in a ponytail. Nor is there a need to be particularly athletic, though it helps. Racing is a few compressed minutes of adrenaline-inducing activity interspersed with long intermissions of sitting, crouching, waiting, and watching.

On a racing boat, there's a variety of roles to suit strength, agility, and ability. These roles can include skipper, tactician, mainsail and jib sail trimmers, and foredeck, which I'll explain in more detail later. Among my assets as a sailor, other than my ass itself, which is useful for ballast, is that at five foot three-and-a-half inches tall, my low centre of gravity makes me comfortable balancing on the foredeck. Generally, there aren't many women who helm or crew on race nights, and even fewer women of colour. Members nod and smile at me in recognition, and I wonder if that's because there are so few Asian Canadian women my age in the community. I'm used to the visibility and foreignness of my body, having attended literary events and art openings for decades where I'd hardly see another Asian woman. I enjoy undoing other people's expectations, and even my own.

I didn't expect to move to Toronto in the summer of 2008—my intention was only to stay a few months. I sublet a room in a Bloordale duplex full of ex-New Brunswick actors and musicians. Shortly after I'd moved in, one of my new roommates invited the household for a sail on a second-hand boat he'd bought the year before. Mark had saved for a year on his "peanut butter and jelly sandwich plan." It turns out that it's possible to buy a boat at the age of thirty by saving for a year, not eating out, and living with roommates, so his oft-told story goes. He's a Maritimer, so tall tales and storytelling are his heritage. Though we'd barely interacted—I was working three jobs at the time—I eagerly responded to his invitation. All I remember of that sail is the evening light on the waves, the laughter of my roommate Amber, her best friend Michelle, and Mark, who was steering us into the middle of the harbour. I hadn't yet made up my mind about living in Toronto, but being on water gave me a feeling I'd been searching for. The next spring, when Mark sent out an email inviting friends and roommates to crew the club's Wednesday-night races, I started showing up. That's how I tell it. I have a sailing story now. And sailing stories are the best stories.

With just half an hour before the race starts, it's time to get off the dock. Amanda and Tim hurry aboard as I step up to the bow to find the mooring lines beneath the weight of the jib. I unhook and hold them taut while Mark starts the motor, and only when he gives me the go-ahead do I toss the lines onto the grass. *Panache* backs slowly out, jostling the boats on either side of us with her bumpers. Other crews wave to us, wishing us a good race and a good time. Some yell out a joke that is lost over the sound of the motor. We keep buoys to port and motor past the Ward's Island ferry dock, where passengers watch us and sometimes wave or take our photo. When we're in sight of the race committee boat, Mark shuts off the engine and tells us to hoist the sails. We pause our chatting to fit the handle into the main halyard winch, pulling and grinding, tilting our heads back to see when the sail reaches the top.

What makes a crew? When do we become a crew? Is it the moment we step onto the boat, performing our various duties? Or is it when we adjust the sails so that they fill out, the boat heeling with the force of the breeze? I'm not sure. I do know at some point I stopped being a passenger. I became— am becoming—a maker of knots, a trimmer of stories.

Free Beer

I WAS SITTING ON the high side of *Panache*, happily swinging my legs, when my slip-on blue Vans sneaker left my foot, arched upward, and plunged into the oyster-coloured lake. Mark valiantly swung the boat around to try to reach it, but the sneaker's white sole eluded us and was added to the inventory of lake detritus. The shoes had cost ten bucks off a discount rack, and I'd worn them because their wavy rubber tread gripped the deck better than my other shoes. It was mid-May 2009 and the first race of the season—it was also my first race ever. I kicked the other sneaker into the cabin and scrambled about the deck barefoot, an auspicious beginning to my racing career. I don't remember if it was chilly, though it must've been. Neither can I tell you the particulars of that race. All I recall is the bright joy of being on a boat again after a long winter, even with a lost shoe.

My memories of those first years of racing are flashes, images lit from behind like clouds passing over the sun. Or like over-exposed Polaroids taped to a wall, pale as faded

T-shirts. Filling in the gaps in my memory are the several years of race and regatta recaps from Mark's sailing blog and the videos he posted to YouTube using a GoPro fixed to the stern rail. It was as if he'd known that I might someday need a record of every time I crewed on *Panache*. My first impressions of Mark are vivid, though—I was wary of his outgoing, restless personality and aptitude with sports and games. His cheerful nature is in sharp contrast to my sarcasm and preference for solitude. Our roommates put up with our constant bickering, but sailing became our common ground. On the boat, I saw Mark differently, as more responsible, quick-thinking, and patient than I'd given him credit for, while he appreciated my work ethic and willingness to pull on any line he pointed out to me. Before he became my roommate, Mark had moved to the city to make or break it as an actor and musician, and it was between auditions and musical theatre gigs that he reconnected with a sport he'd enjoyed as a kid with his grandfather in his native New Brunswick. Mark's blog tracks our mishaps, breakages, hard-won wins, and the gradual improvement of the newbie crew. My sailing story is also a part of someone else's story.

I've heard many times about how Mark contacted yacht clubs in the Toronto area after moving to the city, trying to find one that fit his actor's budget. Rather than ask him to pay hundreds of dollars of associate member fees, Pat Whetung, a Queen City board member and avid racer, introduced him to several skippers who might be a good match for race nights. After crewing two seasons on *Blythe Spirit*, a Viking 28 owned and skippered by Steve and James, a couple of burly, softhearted guys around his age, Mark became a boat owner around his thirtieth birthday. Now he was directing us to toss mooring lines and stow away fenders as he motored *Panache* out of the slip and past the Ward's Island ferry docks. We followed a parade of sailboats heading toward the race committee boat, boats whose names I didn't know yet.

In fact, as Mark's newest roommate, I was still getting to know the rest of the guys on the boat the night of that first race. Quentin: a graphic designer who'd grown up a few blocks away from Mark's family in Fredericton. Steve: from Saint John, who'd performed with Mark in an a capella group during a stint on a cruise ship. Jeremy: a mathematics PhD student and musician from Ohio who lived a few houses down from Mark and me. I was the only female on board, a situation I would frequently complain about, but nonetheless I enjoyed their company. *Panache*'s crew weren't the macho, patronizing type. These roommates and neighbours were the first friends I made when moving to the city. They kept up an entertaining rotation of board game nights, brunches, backyard parties, and improv comedy shows. Sailing felt like an extension of this camaraderie.

Mark's friends had celebrated the purchase of his boat last summer and had made a few outings, but all of us were still orienting ourselves on the 26-foot Niagara. If Mark had doubts about us or his own abilities as skipper, he muted them. He was in bright spirits that we'd shown up, as if drawing energy and amusement from our droll comments and simple questions. We pointed at things, climbed over each other awkwardly, and cracked up over each other's mistakes. Looking back, I have a better picture of why Mark had signed up for the club racing series: the excitement of sharing the sport of racing with his friends, faith that we were smart and agile enough to quickly follow instructions, and knowledge that the best way to learn to race is just to do it.

The Niagara 26 is very forgiving, which in boat parlance means it's a stable vessel that can handle a variety of wind and weather conditions. It isn't a common boat model. Based in Niagara-on-the-Lake, prolific boat builder and designer George Hinterhoeller is most well-known for designing the Shark. The largest one-design keelboat fleet in Canada, the Shark has also been granted its own international class by World Sailing, the world governing body of the sport of sailing. Hinterholler's boats are designed for Great Lakes sailing, and owners in the region refer to their sailboats as "cottages on the water." The Niagara 26 has a fractional rig, tiller, and fin-shaped keel. The mainsheet traveller, which controls the angle of the mainsail, crosses the cockpit and is easily reachable by whoever is on the helm, though it makes the cockpit a little crowded. Mark can also quickly adjust the backstay behind him, which increases or decreases the bend in the mast, a common control on a racing boat. Conveniently lined up atop the cabin are the controls for the cunningham, outhaul, main, jib, and spinnaker halyards, pole lift, and reefing lines. Since our crew didn't know what they were all for, we were liable to flip the wrong clutch handle even though they were clearly labelled. Though I was intimidated by the myriad lines and controls, *Panache* has a straightforward layout. Even before I was familiar with the boat, I sensed that it was more than the sum of its parts—more than merely a deck, hull, V berth, head, sails, lines, and blocks. It was as if someone had tipped a handful of puzzle pieces into my hands, and I saw hints of a bigger image, but I had little idea of how sailing *Panache* would fit into my life.

There are no mentions of sailing in my journal that spring. I was twenty-eight that year, feeling like I had gotten my life back on course after a decade of perfectionism-driven writer's block. I had a lot more on my mind besides racing sailboats. I obsessively dwelled on my unfinished English honours degree and the canonical requirements that left me too depressed to read or write, on my inability to critique CanLit's historical and ongoing racism in my honours thesis, and my dissatisfaction with my poetry. I took myself far too seriously and couldn't navigate away from my guilt and sense of failure. Having moved west for university, I was also disoriented by the coastal climate and Vancouver's curved edges and grids. Though the oceanside campus, the mountain views, and the riot of cherry blossoms each spring were stunning, I was sleepless and low-spirited. Worst of all, I couldn't recognize my own unhappiness and so never asked for help.

I lived at home, tutored, worked in cafés, my degree unfinished. In a mid-twenties limbo and sensing that something drastic needed to change, I packed a duffle bag and booked a one-way plane ticket to Toronto. Soon, the city's energy swept away my depression—there wasn't room for it in the stress of making rent. Working three jobs, I passed out each night after my closing duties and biking home. Fed up with Yorkville customers who spoke as if I couldn't hear the difference between mortadella and mozzarella, I reached another crisis. My mother hadn't put herself through college for me to serve lattes to rude, Botox-injected customers. I applied to school as a mature student and enrolled for the summer semester at York University.

The same week of our first race, I wrote in my journal: "I've put a pause on writing while selecting courses for next fall, and to adjust my thoughts to going back to school, with doubts—is it wise? I am feeling that when it is the right time for writing to be done, it will be—but maybe this is a fallacy. Maybe I need to be forcing my hand." I'd always been prone to a sense of observing my life from the outside. Now the friction of Toronto made me breathless and energized. I saw so many possible paths ahead of me, and all I had to do was pick a direction, steer my way toward it, and hope that I would have enough wind to propel me forward.

I've never been a particularly competitive person and so would've been happy to bob about the harbour without the constraints of a race. I was just grateful to be away from my laptop and notebooks and my third-floor rented room. I had been missing playfulness and fun in my life, and with this motley crew of new friends, it was slowly being injected. Instead of squinting at piles of application forms, rough drafts, and emails, I was gazing at Toronto's steely skyline, the newly dressed trees on the island, and the narrow Eastern and Western Gaps where the waves walk into the lake.

I was eager to be useful but ignorant of how to put my habitual helpfulness into action. I understood that our boat, along with others in our fleet, needed to round the course a set number of times and to do so without any disasters. A child can understand how a race is supposed to work. I craned my head around, admiring the pretty picture the sailboats made with their sails taut. The rest of the crew were smiling brightly at the scene, tasting the spring air. Mark, tiller in hand, was scanning the harbour and making many calculations I wasn't conscious of: observing which end of the start line was favoured, estimating the time it would take to sail the length of the start line, and noting the positions of our competition, all while giving directions to a newbie crew.

The percentage of a yacht club's membership who are active racers varies from club to club, but there are many who prefer cruising—day sails and overnight trips—rather than the fluky and troublesome demands of racing. What might induce a group of lucid adults with hectic professional and social lives to commit one night a week from May to September to turning in circles around a stringent course?

There are no prizes other than club trophies and racing flags made of coloured nylon, and no rewards except another story to repeat with delight and pride. Racers compete for recognition and reputation in a small community. It's a sport that drags you into the present moment and, by doing so, becomes an act of memory-making. Sailors who race are both the actors and the audience. Racing orchestrates constraints that are artificial, that are agreed upon by its participants, who understand that winning is contingent on factors out of their control. It's impossible in recreational racing for the circumstances to be exactly equal. Each boat is advantaged or disadvantaged by its size and condition, the experience of the skipper and crew, and the capricious wind. Nonetheless, strategy, knowledge of racing rules, teamwork, and communication can overcome a boat's racing handicap. Learning, controlling, and improving on these many factors in order to beat boats that are bigger or newer is what makes racing so addictive.

I have heard "beer can racing" used to describe these family-friendly, casual, sunset club races that include mixed fleets and low-to-no entry fees. One of the many origins of this phrase alludes to being able to follow the racecourse from the trail of beer cans in the water. The phrase might also refer to the club's practice of awarding a free jug of beer to the first boat in each fleet to cross the start line. This prize is not a part of the race's sailing instructions and is separate from how a race is officially scored. A skipper can win the jug of beer if the race committee observes their bow over the start line first, regardless of how the boat performs in the race and even if they come in last. When I first heard racers at the club use the phrase "We won the start," it did sound odd. After understanding that getting across the start is the trickiest part of a race, I too think that being first over the line is something to be proud of and acknowledged. If a skipper is inexperienced or knows that their boat isn't fast or big enough to win or even place in the top three, the jug of beer provides added motivation to register for Wednesday-night races. It may not seem like much of a reward for boat owners, who view their boats as sunk costs, but free beer is a great inducement for skippers to exert their starting strategies. Indeed, there are skippers and crew who are more motivated to race by this pitcher than by the flags that are awarded at the end of the season to the boats in each fleet with the best race performances.

Start lines are the most stressful part of a race because of the fear of collision that keeps many boat owners from skippering races. It's incredible to watch multiple boats gathering speed, tacking back and forth below the start line within a few feet of each other, and nimbly avoiding contact. Skippers may jostle for position at the "favoured end," the end closer to the wind, or instead cross down the line to avoid the traffic jam. Other starting strategies include skippers positioning their boats below a competitor's to aggressively push them over the line early, or manoeuvring into a good position at the start line and slowing down by luffing the sails, also known as "sitting on the start line" and much maligned by the rest of the fleet. There's no shame in hanging back a minute or two while other boats cross the start line, and, in fact, that might be a good strategy for inexperienced skippers. They can observe which side of the course has more wind and determine where there is clean air to sail into—wind that isn't disturbed by the sails of other boats. Hanging back was Mark's starting tactic in his early years, as he could also avoid the path of those skippers especially thirsty for their choice of local ale.

Mark once told us the story of a two-person crew at our club who designed their own points reward system for racing. Getting out on the water without mishap: one point. Finding the racecourse: one point. Starting the race: one point. Finishing without breakage: one point. And so on. We laughed at this, because what sounds like a low bar can become insurmountable when your motor dies, halyards get stuck, rolling furlers jam, lines are threaded through the wrong blocks, whisker poles detach, thunderclouds roll in, and the crew is ill or nauseous. I've sailed with older skippers who, after a cancelled or lacklustre race, will say in one breath, "Nothing-got-broken-no-one-fell-overboard!" They'll lean forward to knock their tall cans against mine in a toast, a secular prayer of thanks. Sailors may dwell on every wrong call, on each slow manoeuvre, but they'll also remind themselves that things could've gone much worse.

Mishaps are most likely to happen during the first race of the season, when lines are stiff from months of storage, shackles not properly closed, and crews rusty from lack of exercise. In our case, we hadn't yet acquired the burnished patina of use. With this in mind, Mark had us put on a smaller jib rather than the large genoa, as it would be less onerous for the "untested" crew, according to his log. After practising a few tacks away from the course, we were then deemed competent enough by the skipper to head to the start line. Twenty or thirty boats were tacking back and forth, close enough to hear each other's calls of "Starboard!" over the water.

Because boats of different shapes and sizes all compete in the same race, there are separate starting sequences based on something called a boat's Performance Handicap Racing Fleet. Each boat has an assigned PHRF rating that reflects its model and past race performances. Stars and Sharks start first, then smaller keelboats within a particular rating range, and lastly the larger, faster-rated keelboats. We looked on as the Star and Shark fleets crossed the start. I would soon learn to observe wind conditions and tacking decisions from watching the smaller boats ahead of us round the course. But that first night, my sense of awe at their timing and coordination, and the nimbleness of the crew hiked out on the high side, was all I could attend to. It is an awe that has never left me.

The race committee raised the France flag, which signalled the beginning of our starting sequence. Volunteer race committee members stood in the *Harold Robbins*, an old steel-hulled work boat with short poles along its roof and stern where signal flags can be raised. Large numbers affixed to a board announced the racecourse and the number of times boats are required to go around it. The *Harold Robbins* marked one end of the start line, known as a the "boat end," and a large inflatable orange buoy marked the "pin end." Because the skipper has so many immediate things to pay attention to, it's helpful if crew can find and communicate to them the locations of the committee boat, the starting pin, and the rounding marks. Providing commentary on the race committee's decisions about the course is optional.

The race committee remained stoic as boats veered toward them, sails flapping as they tacked below the invisible line. Any boat that crossed the start line early would be recalled. Since sailboats can't back up, this would entail circling around by bearing off and tacking back to the start line with much chagrin among the crew. To avoid being too early or late to the start line, it's a good practice to designate a crew member as timer, using a stopwatch, kitchen timer, or phone. When the committee boat volunteers simultaneously raised the fleet pennant flag, sounded the horn, and announced the five-minute countdown to the start over the radio, Jeremy or Steve clicked the stopwatch while Mark steered us toward the starting area. Quentin, whose quiet, unflappable demeanour I always find calming, stood in his favourite spot in the hatchway, ready for whatever.

It was only years later that I fully comprehended the story of what happened next. As Mark recapped later, we were out of position a minute before the start and lacked the speed to make it over the start line as our race began, but we were close. The sound of the starting gun rippled toward us and was followed unexpectedly by a second shot. It might've been to signal that a boat was over the line early, but the jib blocked Mark's view and he couldn't be sure. When he was in sight of the committee boat, he was surprised to see them fishing a flag out of the harbour.

It was a new occurrence for him to see the race committee volunteers calling the boats back for a restart, but there is always something new when it comes to racing. He bore off and we waited for the starting sequence to begin again. Despite the instructions coming over the radio, confusion ensued. The bigger boats of the next fleet attempted to start according to their usual sequence. Perhaps the winter break had made them so eager to compete that they felt compelled to head up without the signals from the race committee. After speeding upwind with gusto, they collectively hesitated and one by one returned below the start line. They again attempted to approach the line during our fleet's rebooted start, making it harrowing for us to tack among their wide hulls.

In our fleet, only one other boat had returned for the restart, the aptly named *One More Time*. This was not surprising, as her owner and skipper is Pat Whetung, who was also the club's commodore that year. All the other boats in our fleet, including *Blythe Spirit*, *Sloop du Jour*, *Skeena*, and *Tenacious*, were by this time approaching or rounding the first upwind mark. It was hard to tell if they were aware of the comedy of errors back at the start line. Skippers who did realize their mistake had three choices open to them: abandoning the race, sailing back to the line and having to dodge the boats of the next fleet heading upwind, or continuing around the course only to be disqualified. This last option would, at the very least, give skippers and crew more opportunity for practice, if they felt they needed it.

Mark timed our second start more precisely and was leading on the first upwind leg of his very first race as skipper. While *One More Time* was a few boat lengths behind us, its position kept us pinned on the starboard tack. Unable to tack over, *Panache* sailed wide of the upwind mark while *One More Time* was able to pass us. Despite the C&C 27 keeping a lead on us and ultimately crossing the finish line first, Mark later wrote: "Myself and the crew did have a pretty fun time racing around in second place (in a fleet of two boats who had restarted correctly) and getting to learn the "ropes." When we crossed the finish line without having been protested or having any serious injuries (barefoot Phoebe stubbed a toe), it felt like a huge success."

The race committee takes an hour or two to calculate and post the results on a bulletin board at the clubhouse, which makes skippers cagey about celebrating too early. However, the names of the boats that crossed the start line first are printed and waiting at the bar much sooner. Mark sent one of us to walk upstairs to the bar to check if our boat's name was on the list, to sign for the jug, and to return carrying pint glasses and a foamy plastic pitcher. Whenever I volunteer for this important job, I worry about tripping while carrying it down the stairs, across the boatyard, through the club gate, and beneath the cottonwood trees to *Panache*'s picnic table.

We cheered each other as the spring daylight slowly converted to a blue-glass dusk. Other skippers joined us to complain about the race committee or to admit their error, finding solace in their Koozie-wrapped beers before heading home on the tender or heading up to the clubhouse for more solace. I gradually understood that if *Panache* had been close enough to the start line to cross it with the rest of the fleet, we too might have headed upwind without noticing that the race committee was calling us back for a restart. On the second try, *Panache* was in a better position and sped over the start line. Though Mark couldn't have anticipated the unusual circumstances, it had worked out to his advantage.

Thanks to Mark's blog, I can also chart the number of times I sailed that season. I didn't always show up. Some weeks, I remained at my desk, indecisive about whether to pack my bag. Other weeks, my budget wouldn't allow for the tender ticket or for a six-pack and chips. Some weeks, I felt like sailing was an indulgence when there were so many poems I wanted to write, submissions to send out, jobs to apply for, books to read, chores to do, work to feel guilty about, and inequities in publishing to battle. Every evening spent on the water was an evening away from working toward my independence. I was hardly a writer, hardly settled in an intimidatingly hectic city. I was finally crossing my imaginary start line after years of delays and hesitations, believing I was too late and had distance to make up. I still had to learn how to follow rules I didn't understand, how to strategize the fastest way upwind, and how to maintain my momentum. I still had to allow myself to ask for help. It was many more races before I knew what I could afford and what I was getting for free.

Relative to Wind

EVERY CHOICE OF DIRECTION extends outward from you in a circle of possibility. When leaving the house for a walk, you might head south to the lakeshore, or turn right past the bungalows on your street to a hidden trail through a wooded ravine. Learning to walk as a toddler, you gain balance and move so as not to fall, and then it becomes instinct. You overcome the forces of your own inertia and of gravity. You find your rhythm and momentum when speeding up to jog or run. If you want to change directions, you only need to pivot your hips. Before venturing out, you look out a window or at a weather forecast. You consider your energy. An imminent rainstorm discourages you from your daily walk or a breeze through the lilacs persuades you to strap on your sandals. Unless there's a typhoon or gale, how often do you factor in wind when planning your route?

When you're on land, wind surrounds you, nudges you, and may slow you down, but it doesn't determine your direction the way it does on the water. When you step onto a sailboat, you gain a new sense of the wind's force and direction when the sails fill and the boat skims forward through the waves. It feels like the most natural thing in the world, and you realize that you witness similar forces at work every day, such as a bird gaining height, a piece of paper gliding along the floor. Your senses accept them without needing to know how these objects are governed by laws of motion. Neither do you need to understand physics in order to sail. Learning to tell the wind direction and how to adjust the sails accordingly through trimming them is enough to control a boat's position, direction, and speed.

The points of sail, defined by *The Dictionary of Nautical Literacy* as the "principal headings of a sailboat in relation to the wind," is a circular diagram that shows this relationship between the direction of the wind and that of the boat. It represents the possible and impossible paths that a sailboat can take and is the most fundamental knowledge a sailor uses to orient their boat, to trim the sails relative to the wind, and to reach their destination. Once I understood how a sailboat's position must always take into account the wind's direction, my view of the world and its forces widened even as my paths were limited.

Start by picturing a circle. Imagine the wind coming from the top of the circle, at zero degrees, blowing down to the bottom. Now imagine you're in the middle of the circle, facing into the wind, your hair streaming back. Imagine the resistance you encounter. Let's place your destination upwind, directly ahead but a distance away. We'll drop a mark there, a big inflatable orange buoy on the waves. It could represent a life goal, such as a step-up in your career, a home with bay windows, someone to share your life with. Maybe it's more abstract, such as confronting a trauma or grief. You can see it directly ahead of you. You'll have to use every point of sail— in irons, close-hauled, on a reach or on a run, and everything in between, to arrive at the end of your story. A sailboat race, where there is usually a starting line, finish line, and marks in the water that the participants need to round, is designed so that boats will use as many points of sail as possible. Though it's a competition, in a sense you're racing against your own potential. Other boats might finish faster because they are bigger or their crew more savvy, or perhaps the wind conditions might favour a smaller and lighter boat. Every boat has its limitations and its capacities. Treat the course ahead of you as an opportunity to discover them.

Heading to Wind

When pointed into the wind, there is a no-go zone of roughly forty-five degrees on either side where a sailboat stalls because the sails cannot capture the force of the wind to propel the boat forward. It's difficult to steer when the sails are limp or luffing, resulting in feeling as though the boat is trapped. Another term for this is "in irons," a phrase that is borrowed from the practice of securing criminals on board ships with leg irons.

Being in irons isn't dangerous, unless you're trying to steer out of the way of a possible collision, but it's awkward, frustrating, and embarrassing. Stalling inevitably happens to everyone—like when you tack a boat too slowly through the wind or you aren't concentrating on the wind direction and find yourself facing it head-on. Fortunately, it's a temporary situation. There are many ways of getting out of irons, but the one that most appeals to my passive nature is to do nothing. To wait with the sails eased until the bow drifts of its own accord onto a beam reach. I may be passive, but I'm also patient. When I've been stuck or blocked in my writing, giving myself time for my thoughts to drift is how I find my sense of direction again. I used to stay at my desk for hours and hours, losing sleep while staring down a draft that wouldn't come together. Now I get up, stretch, shower, go for a walk. As I breathe deeply, I can usually see my way forward with the piece.

If you can't wait, another method is to move your weight to the low side, or leeward side, of the boat, inducing heel. Heeling is when the boat leans over at an angle toward the water. It might feel uncomfortable, even nerve-racking, yet within moments you'll feel the difference as the bow slowly turns and the sails start to fill. You'll be amazed at how a slight change in position can make such a difference. Finally, you can push the sails out, otherwise known as backwinding, so the wind begins to push the boat backwards, causing the bow to turn as well. Sometimes you have to go backwards to get unstuck.

Stalling a boat can also be a useful manoeuvre, even a safe one. Skippers stop their boat when the sails are being hoisted or doused, or when something needs to be untangled or repaired. Having the boat even and motionless is best for dropping an anchor and for reefing or dousing a sail in heavy wind. When I took a learn-to-sail class a few years ago, I tacked the dinghy in heavy winds and accidentally capsized. My two other classmates and I breathlessly righted our boat and awkwardly hauled ourselves up. "Can you point us into the wind?" one of the girls gasped. After I did so, we were able to sit under the limp sails and gather ourselves after our sudden cold bath in Lake Ontario. You might find being in irons useful, a zone where you can catch your breath and contemplate the choices that led you there.

Close-Hauled

If the most direct path to your goal isn't possible, you can get there by sailing close-hauled, roughly forty-five degrees to the wind. You can approach the mark at an angle, and if you continue without turning on this path, you'll eventually end up sailing past it. At some point, you'll have to turn the bow about ninety degrees through the wind, also known as "tacking" or "coming about." A skipper can choose either a starboard or port tack, which doesn't refer to the direction of travel but to what side of the boat the wind is moving across. If you're as indecisive as I am, you might look for where there appears to be more wind, or choose a course free of other vessels, so you have clean air to sail into. By tacking repeatedly, the boat makes a zigzag path, which is termed "beating to windward." This is how you can progress toward your destination even if it's directly upwind—by looking ahead, planning your course, and executing tacks quickly and efficiently so you don't stall. Consider it good practice for other parts of your life that require pre-planning and decisive manoeuvres.

When you're sailing upwind, the wind's force on the sail generates lift. A sail acts like a wing. It appears flat, but it is sewn in panels, which gives it a curved shape. Because of the different air pressures flowing on either side of the sail, it receives a force that is perpendicular to the direction of the wind. This should push the boat sideways, but the force of the wind is counterbalanced by the force of drag created by the weight of the keel below the boat working against the water's resistance. As a result, the boat accelerates forward along the path of least resistance. What was my path of least resistance to becoming a writer? To becoming myself? When my days are tightly trimmed, tense with deadlines and obligations, I move speedily toward my goals, but I wonder how long I can keep up the aggressive pace.

Close-hauled is the point of sail that is most frequently used for racing, and the feeling of the boat's speed as it heels is exhilarating. To act as ballast, the crew will move from the low or leeward side to the high or windward side, sitting along the deck with their legs outside the lifelines. You might feel anxious about the boat tipping over and capsizing, but observe its feel and balance. Learn to understand what the sails and the boat are telling you. The more it heels, the more difficult it is to steer, because the rudder is in less contact with the water. Excessive heel causes the bow to turn into the wind, known as "rounding up" or "weather helm." You'll feel pressure on the rudder, so much so that it refuses to stay centred, and you'll be fighting the tiller for control. Some recommend letting the boat turn into the wind, where it will stall, spill wind from its sails, and right itself. Reefing the mainsail so that there's a smaller sail area can also prevent a boat from being overpowered in heavy winds. There are always adjustments you can make to maintain your course in challenging conditions—you are never completely helpless or at the mercy of the wind.

After a lot of work beating upwind, the mark is now only several boat lengths away. You realize that you won't be able to go around it without having to tack again. Not laying or not fetching the mark happens to even experienced sailors, because it's hard to estimate distances and directions when you're approaching your destination from an angle. The wind direction might also have shifted. You can resign yourself to tacking again, and this isn't the end of the world. You can also pinch, meaning you can try to point your boat higher into the wind to adjust its course. But in doing so, you will cause the boat to lose speed and start to stall as it edges into irons. You'll have to consider what your boat can handle, your abilities to steer, your crew's skills.

I have the impression that sailing close-hauled is unsustainable and risky long-term. Sooner or later, a big gust will hit, and if the crew aren't prepared to steer through it and to let out the sails, they could injure themselves, break something, even capsize the boat. I remind myself that boats are designed to be balanced. And that it's tough to know how to handle a vessel or what it's capable of until it's under pressure.

On a Close Reach

Easing the sails slightly away from the wind and turning the boat five to ten degrees from the close-hauled position will bring you on a close reach. A close reach requires less precise trim and steering, and it is more forgiving and manoeuvrable. You are now heading not directly upwind nor perpendicular to it, but somewhere in between. This is a more comfortable angle, with less heel, and yet it's still an efficient point of sail. After changing the angle of the wind to the boat, more of the sail area is exposed to the wind and so this can be a faster point of sail than close-hauled. You'll make fast progress, but you'll end up sacrificing direction, as sailing on a reach is a longer route to an upwind mark.

Unless the wind direction and force are consistently steady, your sails will need constant trimming to find their optimal shape. In heavier winds and with big waves, close hauling rather than reaching may give a faster speed because the boat can slice through the waves, but at the same time, the boat may want to round up into the wind and start to stall. At other times, close reaching may give you more speed because it involves a more favourable angle to the wind. You will need to choose whether to sail faster or sail more directly. You will need to balance speed with stability.

On a Beam Reach

The fastest point of sail on many boats is ninety degrees to the wind, or sailing on a beam reach. This is when the wind is coming across the side—the beam—of the boat. The sails are eased halfway out as the skipper turns the boat, bearing off from the wind. On a beam reach, the boat has less heel, so the crew are more comfortable and in control. If you don't have anywhere in particular to be, or are sailing long-distance across Lake Ontario, a beam reach is the optimal point of sail. Though, eventually, if you want to reach that upwind mark, you'll have to head up again. Sailing on a beam reach is the job you take to pay the bills and keep your pantry stocked with olive oil and rice. It's not lazy or careless—you're moving quickly enough, just not directly toward your goal. You're sidestepping, making a lateral move.

After finishing my MA in creative writing, I couldn't find full-time work, so instead I tutored in Richmond Hill and Vaughan. I sat on the edge of my train seat, worrying that I wouldn't make my connection en route, calculating whether I would make rent that month, how much longer it would take to find a publisher, whether it was still worth it to scrawl poems while the Viva Blue bus bounced up Yonge Street. I relieved myself of the pressure to publish as quickly as possible, to instead focus on the vision of my manuscript that felt most true to itself. I was surprised to be making gains, turning out drafts of poems that sounded as close as possible to what I had intended. By easing up on myself and following my intuition, I set a course toward a more natural and sustainable routine.

On a Broad Reach

On a racecourse, reaching the upwind mark is only half the work, because you're rounding the mark, not stopping at it. After rounding, you wonder why you spent so much energy and effort trying to reach it. But at least now you'll be heading downwind, with the wind behind you—though on a broad reach, the wind is coming from an angle of roughly 120 degrees. If you ease the sails and trim them properly, you'll be able to sail back to where you started. There's less speed on a broad reach, but it's calmer and the boat is flatter, meaning it is standing more upright with less heel. There's time to contemplate what you've just accomplished and how much further you still have to go. Being "on a reach" makes me think of what's within or out of reach—reaching a conclusion, reaching for the stars.

If you think there may be more wind on the other side of the course, you might turn the boat to port or starboard. Turning the stem of the boat through the wind is a manoeuvre called gybing. The boom comes across and the main and jib sails switch sides, so that the boat becomes its own mirror image. There are controlled and uncontrolled gybes. An uncontrolled gybe happens if the wind shifts and the boom flies across the boat dramatically and suddenly, which can be dangerous and may even toss crew overboard. A controlled gybe is planned and deliberate, with crew helping the boom and sails across in a composed manner. You may have realized by now that sailing is all about being in control under conditions that you cannot fully anticipate or change.

The racecourse was likely set by others who strive to make it an enjoyable challenge. The course marks and finish line feel like arbitrary criteria over which you had no control but nonetheless agreed to. You start to question if your other dreams and goals are also subject to limits and conditions. You long to return home to a safe berth where you can sleep and forget the trials of the journey. As the sunset lays its wide hands on the sail, you remember that no one forced you into this course of action and you can abandon the race any time. If the wind dies, if something breaks, if you're tired and not having fun anymore—there's no shame in calling it quits. In the meantime, other boats are coming up from behind and taking the wind, reawakening your competitive spirit. You decide to gybe the boat, determined to see things through to the end.

On a Run

This is the way tall, square-rigged ships sailed when they circumnavigated the world, firing cannons at each other and capturing cargo holds of tea, rum, and china. When Toronto was still known as York, schooners regularly slid into the harbour, but there are few today, other than *Kajama* and her little sister, *Challenge*, that take passengers on a scenic tour of the islands. If the wind is directly 180 degrees behind you, you're on a run. You'll need to ease out all your sails for a long downwind leg. The boom is pushed out until it touches the shrouds, and you put up the whisker pole to hold out the jib. Maybe you'll even douse the jib sail and hoist the spinnaker, a thin, balloon-like sail that resembles a parachute or a kite. This point of sail is also sometimes termed "running before the wind" or "on a dead run," as if fleeing the wind itself. It's not the fastest point of sail, so even with a lot of breeze behind you, going downwind feels leisurely. In the summer, the sweat breaks out on our faces as we sit in the sun after the briskness of beating upwind. We take off our windbreakers and chat idly, our voices drifting out across the grey-blue waves. I think about everything pushing me from behind. It feels like I can coast for a little while, until the boat rounds the leeward mark and we prepare to beat upwind all over again.

The points of sail might not make sense right away. It might take a decade of hustling and juggling before you understand how to beat upwind to take the fastest course toward your ambitions. It might take switching degree programs, schools, and career paths before you're decisive and confident about trying a different tack. You might have to feel a relationship stall, with things unsaid, before you decide to backwind it with a painful argument—or maybe you simply drift out of it.

Metaphors help us make sense of the world, juxtaposing ideas and objects and emotions side by side so that each thing brings understanding to the other. When I learned how to orient myself in relation to the wind, I saw the wayward path of the creative life I'd chosen in a different way. I am less afraid of testing my limits and of letting go of what I can't control. The points of sail are more than a metaphor—they are a way of seeing, of being, that continues to guide me and my imagination.

Becalmed

WE'RE ON A LONG downwind leg when it happens. The jib, held out with the whisker pole and gently billowing, collapses untidily. The main begins to luff, doubting itself. The light air swirls around the boat, no longer giving the lift needed to power the sails. The wind has made a French exit, departing like a shy guest. The midday August sun stares impassively at us. This time of year, at this time of day, is when the wind is most likely to drop. The boat slows, hovers, then stalls. There is something almost offensive about our sense of helplessness. We sit and wait. We squint at the windward mark, which feels miles away, unreachable as an ideal. Nearby crews are, like us, keeping a hand on the swinging boom and pushing away sails in frustration. Becalmed, we're all metaphorically in the same boat. We sit and wait, getting hotter and thirstier. We light cigarettes to note the direction of the trail of smoke. We stretch, take a sip of water, crack open a cold drink, and, like characters in a Beckett play, we grumble when someone hasn't shown up with an announcement.

I can say that Sault Ste. Marie is one of the windiest places I've visited, with a wide, forceful wind that sweeps across its few city streets toward the Lake Superior shoreline. But I can't say whether it's windier than Ottawa, where I grew up, where the winter gales send powdery snow flying over the flat fields. I can tell you that the air in Ottawa, lying in the snowbelt, is crisper and drier than it is in Vancouver, where I went to university. On the west coast, the wind blows the rain sideways, making umbrellas useless, and rattling doors and windows during December storms.

Winds can be classified by regions, by speed and direction, and by other categories. Environment Canada has a wind atlas that shows the mean average wind speeds and wind energy across the country. But looking at these meteorological maps, tables, and charts, I don't get an aggregate picture of local wind conditions in the places I've lived. How we experience wind is relative from morning to evening, from our neighbourhoods to where we work, or where we travel. It's felt in particular microclimates and intervals of time, in that we enjoy a mint morning breeze before August humidity sets in, or that it's windier in Vaughan than it is in downtown Toronto. Not being able to predict or understand local wind and weather conditions makes me feel out of sync and disoriented. I wonder how long I have to live in a place before I can claim to be acclimatized.

Our planet, because of its atmosphere, its rotation, and the sun heating its surface, is a windy place. The world's winds are affected by the Coriolis effect, which deflects the air counter-clockwise in the northern hemisphere and clockwise in the southern. This deflection produces prevailing winds that move above the surface of the Earth. In Canada and other regions in the northern hemisphere at the midlatitudes, the prevailing winds are the westerlies, moving from west to east, in between the polar easterlies to the north and high-pressure horse latitudes to the south. The trade winds, or easterlies, blow in the equatorial region and, as their name suggests, filled the sails of tall ships during the ages of conquest and exploration and formed the trade routes across the oceans. The last of the wind zones are the doldrums, an area buffering the equator with calm, light, and variable winds due to its proximity to the sun.

The air around us is constantly heating and cooling, and periods of apparent calm are only temporary. Our environment may appear still and windless from our vantage point close to the Earth's surface, but the prevailing condition on this planet is motion.

Toronto lies adjacent to a tornado alley that stretches from Goderich to Windsor. This portion of Southwestern Ontario sees a third of the country's tornados each year, which tend to peak in June and July, frequently developing mid-afternoon and early evening. Lake-effect snow occurs when cold air walks across the warmer waters of the Great Lakes and rises into bands of snow clouds. Blizzards will white out the province's busiest thoroughfare, Highway 401, when the wind carries snow from Lake Huron or Georgian Bay. Polar vortices bring a few days of arctic air into the mild Toronto winter. Spring storms send wind racing through the ravines and over the patchwork of neighbourhoods, leaving broken tree boughs lying across roads. The humidex rises throughout the summer, averaging its highest point in September. Blocking high pressure systems cause heatwaves and hours or days of windlessness, during which city dwellers flock to the Toronto Island beaches and give up turning on the stove.

I was born in Ottawa, four hours northeast of Toronto, and so I am used to the long winters of the snowbelt, short springs and summers, and glorious falls. The humid continental climate is one of the many things I find incomprehensible about Toronto since moving here. Flash rainstorms that cause storm drains to flood, false springs, and random fogs that encase downtown—Toronto weather is weird, unpredictable, and entertaining. Friends who were born and raised in the city say the heat from downtown buildings can push rain clouds outward. The tall buildings also create wind funnels, and sailors on the lake have mentioned gusts that travel to the lake from Bay Street, Yonge Street, and University Avenue. I can't find scientific or statistical confirmation for this information, but I believe them. The winds of Toronto are like the city itself, constantly hustling. They may be one reason why, living here, it's so difficult to find extended periods of rest.

The word *doldrums* is derived from dull, and *doldrum* could refer to a slow-witted or dull person. In the early 1800s, if you were in low spirits, you would be described as being "in the doldrums."

But this phrase was also misunderstood to be a real place, and so the meaning was later applied to describe sailing ships that could not advance due to their becalmed condition. Here is an instance when a colloquialism in English became a nautical idiom rather than the other way around. The "doldrums" is named by meteorologists as the Intertidal Convergence

Zone, an area where the north and south trade winds meet. It shifts with the seasons but approximately aligns with the thermal equator. The Zone appears as a ring of clouds and thunderstorms resulting from the proximity of the sun, which creates a humid atmosphere. The heated air becomes buoyant and rises, then expands as it cools, releasing its moisture in a cycle of thunderstorms.

This zone was dreaded by sailors before the advent of steamships. Ships were becalmed for days and weeks, or damaged by storms. Food and water would run low, resulting in scurvy, starvation, and mutiny. Multiple ships' logs from this period detail the doldrums' horrors, as do works of art and popular songs from the period, and literature such as Coleridge's "The Rime of the Ancient Mariner." These traumas could have also deepened our modern signification of "the doldrums" as a state or period of stagnation, a slump, a sense of inescapable ennui, apathy, and malaise. A period when supplies of hope run low.

Sailors can check wind speed and direction on numerous apps such as SailFlow, Windy, Windfinder, Windhub, or Weather Radar. These apps give forecasts based on the Global Forecast System and refresh periodically. I use Windfinder, which is resplendent with features, including a map with coloured bands of knots and mesmerizing white dancing lines showing wind direction. Zooming into Lake Ontario, I see the lines moving in a southeasterly direction across the lake, shifting east across Niagara and Buffalo at a speed of six to seven knots. The app predicts the wind will move in a more southerly direction with a slight increase of wind speed around the lake's horseshoe. It shows the wind direction to the degree, the current wind speed and maximum speed in knots, the weather, temperature, atmospheric temperature, and swell size and period. It's the kind of information a sailor needs in the palm of their hand as they decide what size sail to hoist or what time of day is best to push out on a dinghy. The tiny white flecks move over the terrain on my screen. Above and around me, as I remain stationary, are pressures and forces in constant fluctuation.

Now that I'm over forty, I recognize the signs like an animal that senses a coming storm. The first time I experienced it, in my final year of university, a doctor diagnosed it as a minor depressive order. I wonder if it wasn't merely burnout, brought on by a full course load, my honours thesis, tutoring, a TAship, and, most of all, not having the time or energy for poetry and the grief over the racism inherent in Canadian nationhood and its literary canon. The exhaustion arrives in my body and sends tremors through my sleep patterns, so that I sleep through alarms and lie awake until the smallest hours. Words blur on the page and in my mind, and nothing I read or write feels like it's pinned with any meaning. Headaches swarm and buzz. Bad habits rivet themselves to my routine, and my resulting guilt feels as pervasive as a fly droning in my room. It's not sadness, or anger, but an absence of feeling, like my emotions have been sucked into a whirlpool.

I don't differentiate now between depression, writer's block, and burnout, as they all arise from the same condition: a weary spirit. I experienced it again after my first book came out. I was caught between working two contract jobs, leading high school poetry workshops, contributing to three anthologies, and doing an unforeseen amount of book promotion. I would wake up disoriented and later fall asleep with fears of disappointing others. I identify so strongly with acts of service that it's hard to say no until I'm lying in bed, finally becalmed, wondering what I can jettison overboard to make my load lighter, where I could position my weight to get some heel.

Since I began sailing in Toronto's inner harbour and out on the lake, I have come to expect big breezes in May and air cool enough to require merino base layers and a toque. The wind walks through the island birches and elms whose young leaves are too tentative to act as a barrier. Swirling masses of warm and cool air over the water bring a plethora of cloud conditions, brief showers, and thunderstorms.

This grab bag of weather makes Sailpast, the annual event that officially opens the sailing season at yacht clubs, quite unpredictable. One year, a sudden thunderstorm pounded the docks while the club commodore and board members watched from the restaurant windows. Another year, there was barely enough wind to fill the sails, and what was supposed to be a tidy parade of boats looked instead like a cluttered lineup for brunch in the Annex. May and June usually offer enough wind for races to start and finish, with a few surprises. Rain clouds shake themselves over Etobicoke only to dissipate as the sun starts to lower. Fog squats in the harbour, turning the boats into spectres. Slices of lightning in the evening sky cause the race committee to shorten or cancel the race.

July's long evenings are perfect weather for barbecuing and enjoying the post-race sunsets. As summer advances, the wind drops and the humidity rises like a sticky cake. The air is heated by several million combustions of engines and industry, then funnelled between bank buildings. Environment Canada's *National Marine Weather Guide* notes that tropical air masses travel from the Gulf of Mexico north to Ontario, trapping the cooler air at the lake's surface and causing humidity and mugginess around the Greater Toronto Area.

In August heat waves, I crave an escape from the city's stickiness. I gulp in lake breezes as soon as I'm down by the water. Races are more frequently cancelled due to light air, and even if there appears to be a good breeze in the afternoon, it tends to die down as the sun dips, only, of course, to pick up again after dark, when the boats are in their berths. Strong breezes return in September. Waves are higher in the fall and whitecaps can be seen on the lake, though the water's still generally warm. There can be beautiful sailing days in October, and when those days last beyond the end of haulout, I can't walk out into a warm and windy fall day without feeling cheated.

Sailors can develop Goldilocks Syndrome—I hear complaints about too much wind or too little. A steady wind in the inner harbour can feel like the exception and not the norm. Sailing in gusty winds might damage a boat—a flying boom could injure the crew or sails could be difficult to raise— while light air is barely enough to power the sails and allow boats to finish a race in the allotted time. Queen City members, for example, have nicknamed its race nights "Windless Wednesdays."

Sailors must also consider wind direction. There might be enough of a breeze to sail in, but it could be shifty, rotating from a southerly direction to an easterly one. Or it might stay from the same direction but vary in force, coming in sudden gusts. Sometimes a boat ahead of us catches a lift and speeds toward the upwind mark, only to lose the lead they've gained on a downwind leg after sailing into a "hole"—a patch on the water where the wind drops. Mark, my skipper, has reminded us that the test of a good sailor is to manage and adapt to light air days as well as to gustier ones. I wonder how this lack of consistency has affected Toronto sailors and how much our character is shaped by weather and wind. I've learned to expect the unexpected, to be entertained by the forces that cause us to scramble to reef a sail or to drift idly while watching the lake's surface for ripples, and to be grateful when graced with ideal conditions.

Around us, boats are heeling, but where we are, there's barely enough to fill the sails. In relationships, in education, in work—in any part of life—there can be a sudden loss of momentum. I've found myself in this predicament during the stop-and-go motions of my writing career. Swivelling around to examine the conditions, watching other writers make faster progress, I've felt frustrated and helpless. I look for adjustments I can make, and after uselessly pumping the tiller and trimming my expectations, I've had to accept my delays, however long they might last. In particular, racialized and marginalized writers' careers can stall when editorial boards don't find our work marketable or relatable, only to start to heel once a few organizations move to commit to greater diversity.

The sudden lift of success—invitations, prizes, and recognition—can be both favourable and demanding. Fearful of seeming ungrateful, recognizing the importance of visibility, uncertain whether these opportunities will keep coming, and suspicious of CanLit's tendency to tokenize, writers of colour are often physically, mentally, and spiritually taxed by the strain of keeping on an even keel. From afar, writers of colour who receive recognition might elicit envy and awe for the richness of their work and their resilience, but close up, they're exhausted. Even I, who have not experienced the same level of attention as some of my peers, was drained after the launch of my debut book of poetry in 2017. I wondered whether the invitations came because of the merit of my work or because my identity checked off a box. I craved a lull. I wanted time to catch my breath and look about me to see whether the landscape had really shifted.

From shore, the scene of an evening race may appear serene and picturesque—sailboats seemingly suspended in the rosy sunset, sails gently sagging in a lull, a patch of light air. But close up, the situation verges on chaos, especially when there's wind at the start line and on the windward leg but none at the mark, leading boats of various sizes to crowd together as they try to round. Bigger boats have a larger sail area and longer waterline length, which makes them faster overall and better at holding speed, but their heavier keels make them slower to power up. Smaller boats, such as Sharks, Stars, and J22s, are swifter and more agile, quicker in lighter air. Bigger is not always better. We'll hear stressed-out skippers call, "Overlap!" or "Room!" to indicate that they are owed room at the mark.

The rule is that when two boats are on the same tack when rounding a mark, the leeward boat must keep clear of the windward boat but is entitled to room for a "seamanlike rounding." Think of it as two race cars on a track, where the car on the outside lane cannot push the car on the inside off the track. We'll see smaller Sharks and J22s slip nimbly around the mark between larger keelboats that appear about to come down on them. Somehow, due to the skill of the skippers, collisions are avoided and the boats move tightly around the buoy as if in a groove. Light air, lulls, and holes may be just as dangerous as gusty conditions and require greater vigilance.

Maritime art or marine art, that genre of landscape painting that takes as its subject matter ships and the varied seas, proliferated from the seventeenth century onward in nations invested in seafaring and fishing, particularly in the Dutch Golden Age of painting. The genre of painting contains all the elements that should appeal to me: clouds thick with drama, coastal landscapes, and majestic tall ships that spark the imagination. Yet somehow, few maritime paintings capture my awe. I feel these works lack a sense of intimacy or individuality. Artists of this period chose to render the many-gunned man-of-wars, frigates, and sloops either at a distance, singly, or among a convoy, or else give them a portrait-style treatment. Shown from the vantage point of the shore or some other stationary position, these paintings have a sameness about them. Rarely does the composition show the perspective of the sailors on board, nor are the activities of the crew shown in detail other than a glimpse of a hand reaching for a line or indistinct figures aboard a rowboat. Instead, the painters give a striking impression of the ships' grandeur and the immensity of the sea. Whether the ship is at the mercy of the elements or mastering the waves and wind, these paintings produce a romanticized, sanitized vision of the floating life.

Art historians have linked the frequency and popularity of battle scenes and detailed depictions of warships and ships' portraits with the prestige, wealth, and power of the Dutch colonial navy. This subject matter and how ships are represented call the viewer to the power of the active navy fleets of this period and remind me of how they carried out colonizing policies. These paintings required a large degree of accuracy, especially in the details of ships' sails and construction, and scenes of activities such as boarding, loading cargo, and conducting warfare. Naval officers and sailors who viewed and collected these works were critical of errors, not willing to view artistic licence as an excuse for ignorance. There is something quirky and funny about this fixation with exactitude and correctness, and I can relate to it. At the same time, I find it chilling. To be preoccupied with accuracy rather than how these paintings essentially exalt instruments of war and subjugation demonstrates, to me, an incredible lack of compassion.

My parents are painters, and though they've had many different jobs, they view the world as artists. They arrange their surroundings with an eye to beauty. They love to make things themselves—my dad built hope chests for my sister and me, and our family's dining and work tables, while my mom knitted sweaters for the whole family, sewed matching dresses for my sister and me, and bookbags for my friends' birthdays. They taught us to consider balance, composition, scale, and material, whether we were looking at a piece of furniture, choosing a home, or taking a photo. We were frequent visitors to the National Gallery in Ottawa and spent rainy weekends doing colour studies and painting bowls of fruit on the dining table.

My mother worked as a graphic designer when I was growing up, and she sold her watercolour paintings and prints and jewellery at markets until she owned her own small shop. My dad studied chemistry and worked as a lab technician, then joined my mom when she went freelance. After that, he trained as a custom framer and offered framing services in the gallery shop they ran for a decade in Vancouver's Yaletown. He'd loved art since he was a boy but only started painting in his forties, first attempting oil painting and Chinese brush painting before settling on acrylics and digital prints. Neither of my parents has ever received wide recognition for their work. My mother has the training and discipline, but she lacks ambition and prefers to fill her sketchbook for her own satisfaction. My dad has shown his paintings in community centres and libraries, but I feel he needs to produce much more and to develop his style. Both of them are shy about self-marketing and applying to galleries for representation, no matter how much I urge them to do so.

I used to advise my parents about applying for grants, investing in websites, getting their works professionally photographed, and making portfolios and Instagram accounts, but I no longer subject them to these lectures when I visit. I've accepted that my parents are stubborn and do things at their own pace. I wonder if they would've had more success as artists if they weren't immigrants, if they had stronger networking skills, or if they'd received more support and mentoring.

Seeing their businesses stall, their periods of unemployment and inertia, and their creative lulls has had a profound impact on me. I also have a shy and unambitious character, but as someone Canadian-born, I've had many more opportunities than my parents. They put little pressure or expectations on me, but I still feel like I owe something to the sacrifices they've made for their daughters. I tell people that I'm the least talented but most organized member of my family. Since the age of eleven, I've submitted my work to publications, entered contests, applied to everything within reach. Perhaps I'm less discouraged or fazed than my parents at being becalmed. Perhaps I know better how to steer myself out of a lull.

An English Vessel and Dutch Ships Becalmed, painted by Willem van de Velde in 1660, depicts two ships at eye level—an English ketch with the flag of Saint George hanging limp, its sails barely lifting, and nearby a Dutch merchant ship, similarly motionless. The scene is serene but not void of activity: clouds are caught in their slow drift, while indistinct crew members are occupied with catching on, and a few seabirds skim the nearly still surface. I'm more interested in the story behind this painting than in what it depicts. Despite the fact that ships from the two nations were enmeshed in a series of Anglo–Dutch wars, Charles II invited the father and son van de Velde Elder and Younger to England and housed them in the Queen's House at Greenwich. They established a "factory studio" that was greatly influential, arguably wholly responsible for the British school of maritime painting. It appears that Charles II's economic policies to debilitate Dutch merchant ships did not affect his admiration for that nation's artistic output, nor did the van de Veldes' patriotism hinder them from training a generation of British studio assistants. Did the rulers and subjects of both nations know that art would last longer than war?

In depictions of becalmed ships from this era, there's little sense of danger. The ships are typically presented in a harbour or close to shore. Their becalmed state looks restful and temporary. I'm struck by the sociable atmosphere of the ships in proximity to each other, with rowboats alongside them and crews busy on decks. They reveal that even if the ship is unmoving, those on board are not idle.

These images are close to home, as though the artists' imaginations were limited to the public's desires and fantasies. Perhaps that's the reason I can't find an example of a painting of a ship in the doldrums or one that represents the despair, starvation, scurvy, thirst, and imminent death of sailors stuck in the equatorial calm for weeks. Nor do these works expose the dark side of the Age of Sail—the naval impressment, the practice of flogging and keelhauling wrongdoers on board, the pillaging, the violent encounters with Indigenous peoples, the centuries-long human trafficking during the transatlantic slave trade. These scenes have escaped seventeenth- and eighteenth-century European painters' imaginations, and as a result present instead an illusion and fantasy. As art critic Philip Kennicott wrote in 2018, "Marine paintings are particularly bound up with fantasies of power and dominance that are fundamental to the European and Western sense of self." This idea of self is one that held high the exploring, courageous, patriotic, and enterprising spirit.

In his *Washington Post* review of the National Gallery of Art's exhibit featuring Dutch maritime paintings by Willem van de

Velde the Younger, Simon de Vlieger, Ludolf Backhuysen, and Hendrick Cornelisz Vroom, Kennicott connects the image of the wooden sailing ship with a heroic idea of empire that "elides ideas of discovery and exploration with conquest and exploitation." In his view, these painters are manifesting the tall ship as a metaphor for "ideals of good governance" and "the wise," embodied by the captain whose image satisfies "fantasies of leadership and benign authority." He points out how these works became "a staple in boardrooms and men's clubs" because they functioned like propaganda to prop up naval officers' glorified images of themselves, their victories, their trade, and their nation.

My mind stalls when I contemplate how I might appreciate the artistic accomplishments of Dutch and British marine painters while simultaneously desiring to decolonize this maritime tradition. A ship's portrait is a still life of subjects that are never still, just as a vessel becalmed may appear stagnant while its crew are restlessly tasked, and a nation can celebrate its elided naval history while conscious of its inhuman violence. In images of ships becalmed, warships appear harmless. I cannot see, but I can imagine, the horrors, sufferings, and afflictions of both those subjected to colonial rule and policies and those who carried them out. The imagination, too, is most animate in periods of seeming inactivity.

If there is one painter who lived during the height of Britain's colonial rule who could have had the imagination to capture the suffering of sailors on board a ship becalmed, it is J. M. W. Turner. I can visualize what such a painting might look like, with his trademark tension between stillness and movement, highly theatrical, with a soft yet furious palette. I find Turner's work mesmerizing for the way his use of colour and underlayers can convey churning immensity and skies fiery with light. "I did not paint it to be understood," Turner said of one of his paintings, "but I wished to show what such a scene was." However, Turner preferred painting stormy and turbulent sea conditions and has produced only a few works that depict ships in a becalmed state.

Turner has, however, highlighted the horrors of the slave trade in one of his most famous works, the 1840 oil painting *The Slave Ship*, previously titled *Slavers Throwing overboard the Dead and Dying—Typhoon Coming On*. In the distance, a ship with its sails furled and lashed is tossed between waves, the very opposite of a becalmed state. The sun's white glare tears apart the sky, and in the cacophony of brushstrokes, indistinct figures flail like ash and floating tinder. Turner was inspired by Thomas Clarkson's 1783 book, *The History of the Abolition of the African Slave-Trade*, which narrated the events on board the *Zong*, a British slave ship whose captain ordered 122 sick men and women to be thrown overboard during a typhoon. *The Slave Ship* evoked strong antipathy and admiration from his contemporaries for its subject matter and abstract style and is still debated.

Some see the work as Turner's judgment of the exploitation of human beings as cargo for economic gain, while others critique his aesthetics as distracting the viewer from the content. David Dabydeen has pointed out that the indistinct figures of drowning slaves take away their subjectivity, dramatizing their deaths for the eighteenth-century colonial gaze and for viewers with a latent desire for horror. I imagine that if Turner had painted a similar slave ship in a becalmed state, his obscure style would make it difficult to determine whether he was sympathetic to the enslaved human passengers or was reinforcing their lack of agency.

Trying to reconcile Turner's position by deciding whether his work reproduces colonial violence or critiques it is a false dichotomy. Turner may have had abolitionist sympathies while still being bound by his education and biases. His limitations as an artist are emblematic of the colonial conundrum. *The Slave Ship* cannot capture the lived experience of enslaved peoples, even if it seeks to draw attention to their plight for social commentary. Its incapacities, its obscurity, and its impressionistic brushwork are a demonstration of how European artists, even ones who questioned the ethics of their times, can have a blurry view of individuals and cultures that they have othered and objectified. The painting is not a window into the event it endeavours to represent, but an aperture, a lens widening into the endeavour itself.

In a metaphorical and psychological sense, I need periods of calm, both on the water and off, long stretches to be idle, immobile, or to do the bare minimum. Even the times when I was depressed or burned out, while I wouldn't wish to undergo them again, have served me. I have become more conscious of the limits of my body, more grateful, and more sensitive toward others, especially students who I sense are stuck in an emotional no-go zone. Like the Ancient Mariner and his unfortunate companions, people can be trapped in a becalmed state that is determined not by a specific longitude or latitude, but by actions or circumstances that can follow us anywhere. Unlike Coleridge's penitent narrator, though, individuals experiencing mental distress are not responsible for an unthinking crime or deserving of punishment.

With the close of the Age of Sail, becoming stuck in the doldrums is no longer the danger it once was, and the probability of death, swollen gums, and dehydration in windless zones is much less likely. Yet the doldrums can metaphorically describe the experience of racialization, colonialism, and its resultant grief and intergenerational trauma. A zone that entraps travellers, that brings on starvation, sickness, and a slow death, that necessitates the jettisoning of possessions and assets. This is the position that many colonized subjects found themselves in due to colonialism. Peoples taken hostage and enslaved or pressed into indentured labour entered a kind of permanent doldrums. Generations affected by racist and violent policies may feel as though they're floating backwards, interminably waiting, with little prospect that the wind will pick up in their lifetimes to propel them forward.

Even if the wind is dying, if there are still a few knots floating about the harbour, there's work to be done. In very light air, Mark directs me and other crew to crouch on *Panache*'s low, leeward side to help induce heel. Pat has emphasized weight management and "cat-like" movements to help us to better understand the effects of getting our weight out of the cockpit. Distributing weight to the bow and the low side can remove drag on the stern, and even a slight degree of heel helps the sails to fill out. Avoiding sudden movements can also prevent the boat from rocking and shaking the wind from the sails. One sultry day in July, when there was just enough wind to start a scheduled race, everyone except Mark on the helm and Pat on the main was kneeling along the edge of the boat's low side, trying not to touch the jib. There's little room on *Panache*'s deck between the lifelines and the raised cabin, and after sitting for several minutes, my legs and back invariably cramp up. It felt to me that we were barely crawling forward on the few knots of wind. Then our lead on the rest of the fleet grew and I was astonished, when looking back, that we were half a leg ahead while other boats were still struggling to find wind behind us. We had clean air to sail into, and further upwind, the light breeze held. Although *Panache* had initially been only a few boat lengths ahead, its momentum kept building until, in Mark's words, we "left the fleet behind." We had finished several minutes earlier than even the bigger boat fleets.

Even though our performance that evening should have shown our competitors that managing weight distribution in light wind is a winning strategy, we still see boats with their stern dragging because their crew are sitting in the cockpit. Our bodies are never still and should make the most of continual negotiations with our surroundings, and reacting to lifts, luffs, and changeable pressures.

One Hand for Yourself

SITTING CROSS-LEGGED ON THE bow, I scan the hoop of the lake's horizon. I look down at Mark on the tiller, Quentin standing in the cockpit hatch, Jay being silly. The sun is climbing into a silky blue sky, the motor's been shut off, and the sails are luffing. We're waiting, and the waiting has a stretched and forgetful quality. I don't understand why my fellow crew are seated in the cockpit. At every opportunity, I scramble up to balance at the boat's forestay as the deck rises and dips, calling out any boat that crosses our bow. Did this preference mark me early for the position of foredeck? Does being short with wide hips that help me to balance on a moving vessel make me more physically suited to being on the bow? How does the right position on a boat find each crew member? Through default, or proximity, or choice?

I muse on these questions while gazing at the tearable surface of the water. I'm thirsty and remember I have cold coffee in my thermos down below, but it feels like too much effort to retrieve it. My mind skips to the lyrics to a Destroyer song, the date of my next paycheque, a book I need to review, easy one-pot meals, a yellow yolk spilling itself on noodles. The guys' voices drop off, and my thoughts rush out as if jettisoned from an airlock into a vacuum. But the silence across Lake Ontario isn't a dead one. It's crisp and satisfying, wind-snappy, metal shackles faintly chiming. I look up at the tell-tales on the jib sail and think of nothing. I don't quite reach the solitary vacancy I'm craving, but I come close.

When people ask me how many people are necessary to sail a boat, I tell them it depends. Those who prefer to sail solo can choose a single-handed boat, such as a Laser or Sunfish dinghy, or they can set up a keelboat to be easier for short-handed sailing. The idea of sailing alone with a company of seabirds keening appeals to my romanticism, but it also summons doubts that I could steer a boat in ill winds or handle equipment failure. Still, I picture myself heaving-to and backwinding the jib so I can go below to make coffee, and afterwards resuming my exploration of a lighthouse-studded shoreline. I've never yet sailed without companions, but the possibility lies ahead of me, like a course I haven't set.

Sailing double-handed is a duet that reminds me of playing next to my sister on the piano. Both players have to practise their parts beforehand, though in double-handed sailing, as in music, the goal is to achieve a rhythm together that's more than the sum of their parts. For cruises, couples are the default unit. It's a pas de deux: one skipper on the helm and the other trimming sails, making repairs, dropping the anchor, cooking, cleaning, or sleeping. Dinghies made for double-handed racing, like Albacores, require a choreography of balance and weight. Racing on a keelboat, two sets of hands might be enough for light winds, but on gustier days it can feel like you're juggling too many balls in the air and scrambling for control. With every additional crew member, the roles become more focused. No matter who you sail with, choose your companions with care, as until you're moored and on dry land again, you are literally stuck in the same boat.

In school gym classes, I swayed between apathy and bursts of effort. Sometimes I raced down the field to be open for a pass but grew breathless and frustrated when more athletic classmates overlooked me. As we switched from football to softball to volleyball to track and field, I hoped to show more natural aptitude. I felt graceless trying to dribble or to catch a pop fly, and with every new sport it felt like the same few kids passed and scored while the rest of us jogged lackadaisically along the field. When I was hit in the head by a basketball, knocking off my glasses, my efforts lagged for the rest of the unit. I stopped signing up for gym classes in high school once it was no longer mandatory, as did many of my friends who also accepted that they were bad at sports. We stopped trying, even though our bodies were still changing and growing. When I saw myself as unathletic, it affected more than just my physical activity. I never gained an accurate sense of my endurance and what I might have accomplished with the right kind of practice.

Jobs during a sailing race are typically predetermined—skipper, tactician, mainsail and jib trimmers, and foredeck. Briefly, a skipper is the boat's captain, and their job is to steer the boat, though on a very large yacht, the skipper and the helmsman can be separate positions. A tactician, as the name suggests, advises the skipper on race strategy and tactics, and they might be a former skipper but should have expertise with racing rules and management. A mainsail trimmer controls the position of the boat's main source of power, the largest sail on the boat, which is attached to the mast and boom. Two jib trimmers are optimal on a boat of *Panache*'s size. They set the position of the headsail, the smaller sail at the front of the boat, using lines and the jib winches. Trimming in sailing refers to the act of adjusting the shape and the position of sails using lines, blocks, and winches. While the other positions remain in the cockpit (often referred to as "the pit"), the foredeck crew roams about the deck of the boat. The foredeck crew's tasks are primarily to set the spinnaker or whisker pole that holds out the jib sail when going downwind, and to troubleshoot anything ahead of the mast that the rest of the crew cannot easily reach.

Each of these positions uses different skills and requires a range of experience. On *Panache*, Mark might assign us to positions or ask us to sort ourselves out. "I want to be pulling on things," Tim might say after a few weeks on the foredeck, deciding to help Phil with grinding and tailing. "I don't like being on the foredeck, I don't have good balance up there," Amanda has said, preferring to be on main. There's comfort and familiarity in doing the same tasks from week to week, but I can also start to feel bored. Having crew in the same positions throughout the season is good for *Panache*'s race performance, but at the same time, it's also beneficial for crew to move around. It gives us a better understanding

of how to make the jobs of our fellow crew members easier. Having tried trimming the mainsail in heavy winds, for
instance, showed me the importance of calling gusts from the
foredeck. There is nothing about sailing I'll refuse to do, only
things that I find harder or scarier than others. Yet it's these
difficult, intimidating tasks that bring the most satisfaction
when I accomplish them. Spending too much time in a place
that feels safe, effortless, and painless ultimately leads me to a
sense of disquiet, just as any smooth line, rubbing constantly
against a fairlead or block, will eventually start to fray.

Memorizing formulas and theories. Making quick decisions.
Running long distances, or even sprinting, unless it's for a bus.
Negotiating. Not overwatering houseplants with waxy leaves.
Strategizing, whether in a board game or in my career. Being
consistent in any kind of exercise regimen, sleep schedule,
or diet. Hiding my irritation or contempt. Calculus, or any
kind of math where there are more letters than numbers.
Organic chemistry. Swallowing my pride and asking for help.
Getting rid of the chip on my shoulder against those who are
more privileged than me. My chess endgame. Letting insecure
or needy people take up too much of my emotional band-
width and being unable to refuse them help and attention.
Boundaries, in general.

I'm not terribly strong or flexible. I never learned to drive
and have no knowledge of engine repair or how to fix a flat.
I have little knowledge of first aid or self-defence. I have an
aversion to, but not a phobia of, heights. For a long time, I
was mired in loans and debts, and so believed that I wasn't
good with money. I've never tried any of the following: skiing,

snowboarding, hang-gliding, bungee-jumping, diving from a board higher than a metre, parachuting, rollerblading, or skateboarding. From this list, I conclude that I'm generally risk-averse, or that I don't seek the kind of thrills that only prove what I already know about myself.

The word *skipper* derives from the Middle Dutch word *scipper*, from *scip*, a word that also occurs in Old English, meaning "ship or boat," and means "captain or master of a ship." It's fitting that the etymology of skipper makes the captain synonymous with the vessel. Crew can be particular about sailing with difficult and demanding skippers or, as I've heard them described, Captain Ahab types. Overhearing the shouting from yell-y skippers on other boats and witnessing flustered crews, I'm grateful for Mark's laid-back style. His requests to prepare for a tack or gybe are sometimes so hard to hear that I make a running joke of his mumbling.

What I did understand, without having to ask, was that it was important not to challenge or object to any skipper's instructions—not only is it rude, but it can also be potentially dangerous. Maybe it's human nature to respect authority and to create hierarchies. I like to think that we don't merely respect Mark because of his position as a boat owner and skipper but because of his experience. If he ever asked me to do anything unsafe, I'd be comfortable refusing. Respect is given to those who permit the possibility of disrespect. There's only room for one skipper on a boat, but they are only as good as their crew.

I remain convinced that I'm not a natural skipper, if such a thing exists. While observing others on the helm, I feel they have a confidence I lack, a decisiveness in their movements, even an aggression. Whenever I take the tiller, it feels like grasping a live thing: the slight delay whenever I pull or push the tiller, which is connected to the rudder, the force of water streaming against the rudder, and then the surprising responsiveness. Steering a boat with a tiller is counterintuitive: the boat turns in the direction opposite the tiller's movement. The sails would luff whenever I was distracted by a conversation and let the tiller drift. Even with the entire harbour to bob about in, I had a hard time staying clear of island taxis. I'd spin or stall, or accidently toss my companions around the cockpit when the boat suddenly heeled. I didn't take the helm often enough for my steering to become automatic, and I had to concentrate and constantly correct. Gradually, I learned a few tricks—to find a landmark on the horizon, like the CN Tower, to point toward, and to look up at the wind indicator at the top of the mast or the compass. Every crew member should learn to steer, in case the skipper is ill or simply needs a break. More and more often, after we cross the finish line, I ask for a turn on the tiller.

Yet I still have no desire to be the one calling the shots in a race. It's too much responsibility. I can't fathom how it could possibly be fun, though it must be, because otherwise no one would step into such a leadership role. Faced with the choice of where to cross the start line, which side of the racecourse to beat upwind, when to tack to the layline, I would succumb to decision fatigue. This is why having a tactician is so valuable—someone who observes what the competition is doing, advises on what course to take, and ensures that the skipper is following the rules of right of way, so they can focus on steering the boat. I believe a skipper should always remain cool and collected, even if someone releases a jib sheet too early or if another skipper attempts to barge the start line behind them. No one likes being yelled at, but neither do I want to be the one doing the yelling. People know me as having a calm and grounded attitude, but I don't know if that would last long under the stress of helming. I don't want to discover in myself a capacity for tyranny.

I have been let go from several jobs. The theatre on Dupont when I never quite mastered listening to attendees' requests while clicking the tiny boxes on the ticketing software. An ESL school when I couldn't summon the charisma or confidence to hold students' attention. But I liked being a server—to meet people's needs so immediately and concretely filled a void in me. Remembering to fill their waterglasses, how spicy they wanted their chicken curry, how much hot water they preferred in their Americanos. What I liked best was to clean machines, peel vegetables, or, at dawn, after disarming the café alarm, follow the exact same routine in taking the croissants out to prep, starting the bread machines, brewing coffee, setting out patio furniture, and turning on a soundtrack of the Be Good Tanyas, Iron & Wine, Bessie Smith, Broken Social Scene, Wilco, Sufjan Stevens, Lead Belly, and Neil Young. I went through the motions while my mind walked down to the water.

Manuals on sailboat racing describe crew positions in a highly technical manner, but I can't find descriptions on what the experience is like. For instance, when explaining the role of

the mainsail trimmer, the manuals begin by diagramming
and labelling the parts of the mainsail. From these diagrams,
a reader can see that the top of the sail is called the head, and
the bottom edge is called the foot. The luff is the front and
leading edge of the sail, and the mainsail's luff lines up with
the mast, the jib sail with the forestay. The leech is the back or
trailing edge of the sail. The corners of the sail also have names:
the front corner is called the tack, and the aft corner is called
the clew. The bottom of the edge runs parallel to the boom, a
long aluminum spar with one end attached to the mast and the
other end attached to the mainsail. To help you remember its
name, "boom" is the noise it makes when it clangs against your
forehead. Sails also have battens running parallel at intervals,
which give the sail structure, and mainsails also have reefing
points above the foot so that the sail can be lowered in high
winds and shortened by tying straps through its eyelets, which
reduces the sail area. What the manuals tend not to explain
explicitly is that by learning these terms, the trimmer grows
more attentive to each part of the sail and its shape.

Here's what it feels like to trim the main: When I stand
below the enormous and grand piece of precisely cut Dacron,
laminate, Kevlar, or carbon, I feel excited at the prospect of
trimming the boat's main source of power. I uncleat the
mainsheet, which attaches from the boom to the mainsheet
traveller, and I feel the force of the wind and the tension on
the heavy line. From its centre position, the boom can swing
nearly forty-five degrees in both directions, until it's stopped
by the shrouds. I can change this angle by easing the mainsheet, or releasing it and paying out the line, or sheeting it
in, which brings the boom and the sail back to the centre-
line. Trimming the main requires focus, requires staring up

at the shape of the sail and feeling the heel and speed of the boat. I can easily become fixated on the sail's wrinkles and the telltales, which are bits of tape or yarn attached to the sail at intervals that indicate the flow of air on both sides of the sail. When I have only one job to do on a boat, I relish the telescoping of purpose, the temporary sensation of time blurring. Afterwards, I'm surprised at my tired arms.

I also enjoy how the twist of the sail can be adjusted with the mainsheet traveller. By moving the mainsheet tension block on a track, the angle of the boom can be moved toward or away from the wind—but here I am getting technical. Once someone has learned the basics, it's easy to delve into the ways sail shapes can be fine-tuned. Upwind and in heavy air, the sails should be flatter, and downwind and in light air, the sails should have more curve to catch more air. There are various controls to adjust the mainsail, like the boom vang, which adds tension to the mast; the outhaul, to ease or flatten the sail from the clew and add depth to the foot of the sail; and the backstay, which can add or decrease mast bend. They're used for the endless small adjustments that optimize the shape of the sail so that the boat can go incrementally faster; those increments can make a big difference over time and distance. Trimming sails brings out the detail-oriented side of my personality, the dissatisfied perfectionist. There's so much satisfaction in centring the boom and slightly sheeting the main in and feeling the boat respond immediately. For every action there is a reaction, even if I can't immediately see it.

Jib trimmers are the meat and potatoes of the crew, doing the grunt work of switching the big genoa or smaller jib from one side of the boat to the other. When the boat tacks (turning the bow through the wind) or gybes (turning the stern through the wind), the jib trimmers launch into a flurry of activity. As the skipper begins turning the boat, the trimmer uncleats the "working" sheet, then grabs the "lazy" sheet, wrapping it around the winch clockwise two or three times before hauling it in, bent over the winch to duck under the swinging boom while their hands move blurredly as the jib switches sides and before it fills out. Jib trimming can be a two-person job, especially in heavy winds. One jib trimmer might use a winch handle to bring the sail in while the other trimmer yanks on the tail end of the line, a manoeuvre known as "grinding and tailing." As the headsail begins to fill out and the boat accelerates, they will trim the sail by either easing it out or sheeting it in until the telltales or ticklers are flying. Depending on the amount of wind and force on the sail, this requires either heaving or light tugging. Becoming a good trimmer necessitates becoming a reader of wind.

I have difficulty with reading ticklers, which are sewn on either side of the top, middle, and bottom thirds of the sail. Ideally, they should be streaming steadily back and not hanging limp or flying upward manically. These ticklers can indicate how well the boat is pointing and whether it is pinching, or sailing too close to the wind, but I haven't yet reached that level of tickler literacy. Instead, I follow the mantra of "trimming to the edge of the luff," and "when in doubt, let it out," which means to let the sail out until it begins to luff and then sheeting it in until it isn't. In very light wind, my own technique is to unwrap the jib sheet from the winch so I can feel the immediate pressure on the sail when it's trimmed correctly or the slack on the sheet when it starts to bubble or luff. Sail trimmers make the most of the wind they're given, whether it's a steady, favourable breeze or changeable, fickle puffs of air. There's always the possibility, or inevitability, of finding a different angle of approach.

On hot summer days, my parents filled a kiddie pool in the backyard. There are photos of me at the age of four, splashing with buckets of water, and my mom says I'd spend hours in my bathing suit. I'd run toward any beach and wade with arm floaties until I was called out. As soon as we were old enough to stand in the shallow end, our dad took my sister to the Plant Bath pool a few blocks from our house in Ottawa, at the intersection where Little Italy and Chinatown meet. In university, swimming slow breaststroke laps two or three times a week was a relief from reading. I crave the meditative circuit and being horizontal when I'm away from the pool for too long.

Growing up, my sister and I took ballet lessons, thwacked birdies with our badminton rackets in our driveway, and played skipping rope games throughout elementary school. When I look back, I see myself skating and tobogganing, tearing across the park next door, skipping along Gatineau trails with my parents, and realize I was an active child. I couldn't resist a hidden path or unfamiliar park, always running to discover what was through the trees. This activity slowed when I became a bookwormish teenager, and I didn't learn to bike until my twenties. When I visited my sister in Halifax during her art school years, she urged me onto a mountain bike in a Sobeys parking lot, shouting, "Pedal! Pedal!" until I balanced out of sheer panic. I hit bumpers on too-wide turns and bruised myself against car mirrors. Even so, my sister applauded how quickly I learned. After that, I sped joyfully down hills in Vancouver or through Toronto's grid at night, delighted with the freedom of choosing my own pace and route.

I still spend a lot of time in inactive and sedentary positions, so to move my body is to launch myself into the present moment. It's the opposite of reflection. Swimming, biking, kayaking, and sailing—I prefer exercise that doesn't feel like exercise, that is scenic, an endless loop.

Foredeck can be a lonely position, as I'm too far forward to hear conversations in the cockpit. But it's a position that rewards my love of observation. Sitting forward on the bow, I can watch the drama of the starting sequences and use the boats ahead of us as indicators of how much wind there is on the course. I can peek below the sail at boats on the same tack or watch them coming from behind. I can call out my sightings of marks and the distance in boat lengths, warn of wakes and debris in the water, and relay information about lifts and gusts ahead. Or I might tuck away a view of evening, pink-dyed sky like a handkerchief in my memory to recall later.

I don't think there is anything extraordinary about setting a whisker pole, but others comment that I make it look easy. On a downwind leg, the sails are trimmed so that they are nearly perpendicular to the boat's hull and the wind fills them from behind. As we approach the windward mark and the skipper prepares to bear off, they will communicate whether the jib sail will be moving to the port or the starboard side.

When I hear "Pole on red!" I unhook the long, aluminum whisker pole that lies alongside the deck. Its function is to hold the jib sail out so that it keeps its shape better, with one end attached to the mast and the other to the corner of the sail. The telescoping pole is over twice my height in length, and holding it across the deck, I feel like a medieval knight about to joust. I manoeuvre it so that it's horizontal and perpendicular to the deck, one end forward of the mast and the other extending out. I tuck the pole under my arm while reaching for the jib sheet with one hand and open the pole's hook latch so I can jam in the sheet. At this point, I run out of hands to keep myself on board, so I need to act fast. Once the pole is on the line, I'll push the sail so it can fill out while I attach the other end to a metal ring on the mast and adjust its height. Then I'll grab the centre of the pole to scope it out and twist-lock it, completing the pole set. I'll rush around to the front of the main that has been eased out and push the boom forward until the mainsheet is taut. Depending on where my weight needs to be, I'll sit pushing on the boom to keep it from flying across, alongside the poled-out jib, or forward on the bow. Sometimes I'll have help, sometimes I won't.

As with most jobs on the boat, what takes me a paragraph to describe in writing needs to happen as quickly as possible. On downwind legs, boats lose their speed and are slower to steer, and we can gain an advantage if I can quickly pole out the jib. On sunny, light days, this task can feel leisurely. The boat is flat and easy to grip with the tread of my boat shoes, and I can balance without grabbing onto a shroud or sinking to my knees. On sodden, windy days, however, I'm nerve-wracked just contemplating the manoeuvre. Dreadful images of dropping the pole overboard, taking too long to wrangle an unruly jib sheet, or slipping on the deck swarm my brain like tiny sparks. But when the time comes, I start moving as if my body's sureness might trick my mind.

I'm uncomfortable with comments about my talent, as if talent is something inherent. I'm suspicious of ulterior motives, such as people buttering me up for a request or a favour. I blame this on a lack of praise from my parents. Whenever I showed them a drawing or story, they pointed out what could be improved. They weren't unloving but showed their care through criticism. I remember nurses who praised my stalwart reaction to being injured, dental hygienists who called me the "perfect patient." A co-worker who admired my ability to "not freak out." ESL students who liked my explanations and examples, friends who relished my dumplings and steamed ginger and onion bass, a fellow poet who paid me the compliment of writing about my work. My sister, who credited me with teaching her how to read and to swim. In fact, my Chinese name, 嘉懿, means "to work hard and receive praise," a definition I'm only half-comfortable with.

The old adage that a good man is hard to find can be applied to crew as well: good crew are hard to find, and hard to keep. At the club, I hear skippers sigh over this continual problem. Life itself is the cause of crew attrition—people get too busy, move away, have families, lose interest, or take up other hobbies. Kids who sailed with their parents might buy or begin racing their own boats. At the same time, I meet countless people eager to try sailing, curious about how to get in touch with skippers. It seems like an easy fix to match them up, no?

Unfortunately, it's not. Boat owners who race are only a small percentage of any club membership; the majority are cruisers, who prefer to enjoy their boats with their partners and family. So it can be difficult to get an invitation to sail unless you know someone. Skippers who race don't invite everyone and anyone to crew with them, or, I should say, some of them do and some of them don't. Some only want sailors who are experienced, who stay calm under pressure, and who can put aside their egos to follow instructions. Others just want to sail with anyone who's good company. A lack of experience might be appealing to skippers who are happy to mentor and train new faces who haven't accrued bad habits.

I have often thought there ought to be a matchmaking app for skippers looking for crew, and vice versa. Most clubs do have a membership chair who can connect skippers and crew, or a crew bank consisting of an online message board, or a sign-up sheet posted at the club for each race. The most efficient way for skippers and crew to find each other on short notice is to stroll through a club, making requests in a game of boat-telephone. As long as you start and finish the race with the same number of crew members, it's never too late for someone to hop aboard, even if the boat is halfway out of the lagoon.

Mark says that good crew are those who show up every week. For the first few seasons on *Panache*, our crew was a rotating cast of characters. There were recurring faces:

Quentin, Jason, Phil, Perry, Frankie, Kristina, Jake, myself, and many others who crewed for a few seasons and moved on, but Mark rarely had the same combination of crew members from week to week. Some nights he scrambled to find willing bodies after a flurry of cancellations and no-shows, asking other skippers with a surplus of crew whether he could relieve them of a spare member, while other nights he himself was overloaded with more eager than experienced bodies. Even Mark's social nature was taxed by this continual management of family, friends, roommates, friends of friends, neighbours, co-workers, musical theatre colleagues, strays, and strangers. Because of his crew's unpredictable schedules, Mark was not only the skipper and helmsman, but a tactician and mainsheet trimmer as well. He has said that he finds it difficult to teach the crew when he's concentrating on the race, but he literally had his hands full because the rest of us didn't show up often enough to learn other positions and to do them consistently.

Panache's racing career might be divided into two eras: Before Pat (2009–2012) and After Pat (2013–present day). After retiring *One More Time* from over two decades of successful racing, Pat had chosen the crew of *Panache* to mentor and joined as a tactician and mainsheet trimmer. In her opinion, he was doing too much and his only job should be to drive the boat. Pat was in her sixties when she began crewing with us, and a natural teacher. Mark now had someone with experience who understood the complexities of race strategy and whose voice was loud enough that she amplified Mark's commands so that even on the bow I heard them. In ensuing years our communication improved and we became what Mark called a "well-oiled crew." We required less instruction from

Mark and our manoeuvres had become clockwork-like. By 2020 and during the pandemic, Mark had finally achieved the regular crew that so many skippers covet. At that time, we limited the crew to a social bubble of just six of us. Along with Mark and Pat, there was Phil, a truck driver and dispatcher who was strong enough to grind in the jib on his own and had shown up at the club in 2012 looking for a boat to crew on; Tim, a half-Asian engineer and a friend of Mark's younger brother, and who became an extremely versatile crew member; and Amanda, who I met in grad school and was the only person I managed to recruit from my many friends who had expressed interest in sailing. Amanda is also an Albacore dinghy sailor at one of the outer harbour clubs and so could helm the boat during the Women's Skipper Race. In 2023, when Tim moved to Europe, Mark invited two new associate members, Jade and Tala, to join the crew of *Panache*. None of us needed constant urging and reminders from Mark to show up, because it is only by showing up week after week that crew members learn how to find one another without having to look.

Working as a server, I put a uniform over my shyness. I didn't really enjoy my personality and I was too much in my head, self-conscious, blunt, and opinionated. My co-workers cared less about my personality than whether I remembered a customer's order and pulled my weight in cleaning the machines. They liked me if I was quick and efficient, if I shortened my break when they had a sudden rush. It was a relief too to not have to think of conversation topics, nodding when the head waiter gave one of his Cantonese monologues about life or when a co-worker who regularly took marijuana for migraines detailed the cause of her chronic pain. I have always enjoyed being part of a choir, band, or cast rather than standing onstage alone. I like the camaraderie of circumstance.

Someone who comes aboard *Panache* for a race with no previous knowledge of sailing will be told by the crew to only observe and to act as ballast, moving their weight from side to side as the boat tacks and gybes. This allows them to become familiar with how the boat feels and to enjoy the view from the middle of the deck. It takes time for their senses to adjust to the new information they're taking in. "Stay on the boat," Mark exhorts, hoping that this reminder will keep guest crew from falling off. Phil recommends checking that they don't sit on any lines, and I point out the lifelines and handholds.

Seeing us hoisting sails and trimming them, they invariably ask what they can help with. If they seem eager, they might be assigned to help Phil with jib trim, and if they keep showing up for races, they'll learn how to release and pull in the jib sheets. If they show a talent for observing the wind direction and optimizing the sails, the skipper can assign them to trim the main. Or, if they have a good sense of balance and can see potential problems before they happen, they could join me on foredeck. At any time, they could take a dinghy or keelboat class or buy a sailboat and become a skipper themselves, training their own crew.

But to start off, they'll be given simple tasks, which they'll do without understanding how every adjustment affects the boat's heel and speed. They haven't yet learned to put their face into the wind to track its direction, or to feel the degree of incline in the hull beneath them when the boat picks up speed. I watch them watching without comprehending what they're seeing. I watch them face the wrong direction, not realizing how they might be blocking the wind. I see their curiosity and their pleasure, and I wait for that slow opening of awareness that rewards their interest, as it did mine. We all start out as ballast.

If it's not obvious by now, the skipper and the crew need to work in tandem. For instance, when the skipper begins to bear off, turning the boat away from the wind, the main and jib trimmers should ease out the sails. An autonomous crew that automatically and properly trims the sails as the skipper steers can save time on the racecourse. This is why there's such a void when one good, experienced crew member is missing. They become indispensable, even irreplaceable. I think there is something beautiful about crew members' reliance and trust in each other, but I'm uncomfortable with believing myself to be a vital part of a crew. When I've been out of town for races, Mark has told me that I was missed. I've been horrified to hear that my replacement on the foredeck felt they didn't measure up to some non-existent standard, and I've scolded Mark and told him that's both bad for crew morale and untrue, as I've made plenty of mistakes on board. We all have, and even though my mistakes bother me, I'm grateful to have had the chance to make them. Becoming crew also means being okay with occasionally letting people down.

Many of our wins and losses come down to a matter of minutes and seconds, which makes me increasingly conscious about how much time my mistakes might cost us. Even though the races are meant to be fun, even though blame is never assigned to anyone's lack of know-how or to slow reactions, I still don't wish to be dead weight. Whenever I wrapped the jib sheet the wrong way around the winch or became tangled in a line, I breathlessly apologized and chastised myself for the rest of the race. Whenever I couldn't hook the whisker pole on or when I struggled to push the flapping genoa over, I felt like the seconds crawled. I began rewatching the YouTube videos Mark shot of our races using a GoPro attached to the rail, and I saw how I would literally rock the boat by leaning and craning around the sail. Afterwards, I forced myself to sit calmly on the deck, to move lightly across the bow, and to crouch still on the leeward side until my legs cramped.

There is one video from a race in 2013 that I couldn't bring myself to watch for many years. The Champions of Champions race was our reward for having finished in the first three places overall in at least one of the series of Wednesday-night races. It takes place on a Saturday in late September, when the water in the harbour is still warm but the wind is changeable due to the fall's meeting of warm and cool air masses. "We sailed three five-lap races in the most 'Toronto harbour' sailing conditions possible: north wind with tons of gusts and lulls and constant shifts," wrote Mark in his blog recap. We were also shorthanded, with only Pat, Meg, Mark, and me present. Five times around over three races meant having to set the pole fifteen times as we sped up the course, powered by gusts, only to sit in lulls when the wind suddenly decreased. By the end of the three races, my arms ached. The video shows me unable to release the whisker pole from the jib sheet at least twice, costing us a minute here and there as the pole jammed itself along a lifeline and dipped into the water. Whenever I'm praised now for my speedy pole sets or overhear comments about other crews members' lack of ease on the foredeck, I remind everyone that I wasn't always as quick about my business.

Rewatching the video now, I hear Mark calling for the jib sheet to be hauled in before I got the pole off, and in doing so, the edge of the sail and the end of the whisker pole moved out of my reach. I didn't know back then to yell out that I needed the sheet to be eased, which still would've cost us time, but less than it did with me scrambling to free the pole. Despite these delays, we still placed within the top three in each of the races, winning our last race and placing third overall in the day's results.

I watch myself moving unhesitatingly, the wind whipping around me as I strain to scope out the pole to its maximum length. Pat and Meg frantically pull in the mainsheet and jib sheet, bouncing back and forth across the cockpit. Meg usually sailed on *Ace*, one of the many 24-foot Sharks at the club. I admired her toughness, capability, and sense of style. Unlike me, she saw what jobs needed to be done without constantly checking in with the skipper. As we sat savouring the fact that we had actually completed the races without breakages or major injuries, she saw my torn, bleeding hands and nails. "What a trooper," she said, the approval in her voice a sudden and unexpected windfall.

There is a saying that goes, "One hand for the boat and one hand for yourself." It's a reminder, especially for crew members who tend to prioritize the boat's performance over their own safety, to always hold on to some part of the boat. It might not be with my hands—I can hook my elbow around a shroud, or wedge my foot against a stanchion, rail, or cleat. I have never fallen off the boat (knock on wood) and I might have a hubristic confidence as a result. I've slipped only once, while trying to get the pole onto the mast under strong wind. It was during an AHMEN race, an interclub series on the lake, and the last race of the season in October. The lake was heaving and spraying itself all over the bow. The deck was wet, my shoes were wet, the pole was wet, and while wrangling it, I lost my grip and my legs went out from under me. I fell close to the centre of the foredeck and so didn't roll off. I got up and once again seized the pole as Mark and the others back in the cockpit watched, aghast. Another crew member was on the foredeck with me, and he urged me to let go of the pole. I knew there was so much force on it that he wouldn't be able to attach it on his own, and I ignored him. The pole hit me in the forehead before the two of us were able to attach it to the mast. Even now, I can still feel the bruise on my head, that soft patch. I take pride in my ability to get up again and to keep trying until the job's done, and my racing experiences have shown me that I can accomplish more than people expect. I wonder what I have left to prove. What I should be holding on to to keep me centred.

I like folding copies of my poems into envelopes and slipping them into mailboxes, addressed to magazines and literary journals around the country. I like the idea of the poems fending for themselves, of having no to little reputation that might influence the editors' decisions. I want what I made, and not myself, to receive acknowledgement. The fallacy in this desire is that I wasn't in control of the conditions that engendered my writing. Opportunities were placed within reach—my parents' library of worn paperback classics, a plethora of school gallery and museum visits, poetry workshops and guest speakers and theatre tickets within as close reach as the elm tree outside my window. If I wanted to lie on my bed all summer afternoon reading *Emily of New Moon* or spend my allowance on a blank notebook, I was free to do so. Did I need someone to tell me I was doing a good job? For a long time, I thought I did, only to find that the result wasn't as important to me as the effort. Though it's nice to be told, all the same.

The Badlands

I BRUSH OFF ANOTHER sticky bud from the picnic bench and sit down. The grove of cottonwood trees beside the Algonquin Bridge is prolific, scattering thousands of resinous catkins each late spring over the lagoon, boats, dock boxes, BBQs, tables, and lawns, staining decks and clothes with a yellowish resin. In this area of the club, there are always a few brooms lying about, and if I'm feeling keen, I'll sweep the buds off *Panache*'s deck before we head out. Later in June, the female cottonwoods bear tiny fruit, their branches dripping with bunches of small green beads that harden and burst. Inside are hundreds of seeds that fly out on cottony fibres, giving the tree its name. These fluffies stick to lines, halyards, and cleats, clog the water, and fill the air like soap suds. Once again, we get out brushes and brooms, irked at the mess. But it's fruitless. Only when we get out onto the lake do the buds blow off cleats and blocks.

This area of Queen City, stretching from outside of the south gate alongside the houses on Algonquin Island toward the bridge, is nicknamed "the Badlands." The origins of this name are unknown, but one story is that the city had dumped a load of oily-smelling mud dredged from the harbour next to the lagoon, and the smell made it an undesirable location to moor a boat. The cottonwoods that eventually grew on this mound of dredgeate didn't make it any more attractive, because they are messy trees. Their wood is brittle and weak because they are so fast-growing. After windstorms, twigs and branches are tossed about like old clothing. Its wood is often used in chipboard and plywood—it's possible the boats and club buildings contain cottonwood. They are more appreciated by wildlife such as beavers who build houses with their branches and squirrels who snack on their catkins. Traditionally, cottonwoods are an indicator of water because they can be found along streams and riverbanks. It can be hard to distinguish them from poplars and aspens. They have triangular, unremarkable leaves and greyish bark. Though they are nondescript, they are impossible to ignore.

It's *Panache*'s week to barbecue, so our crew has carted over enough sausages, veggie dogs, sauerkraut, buns, potato and beet salads, chips, and snacks to feed the crews of four or five other boats docked in the Badlands. After the race, Mark fires up the grill and we prepare to feed the ravenous sailors around the picnic tables as they endlessly replay the starts, roundings, close calls, fouls, and finishes. I barely understand their recaps—I've only been racing a few seasons, and I'm in awe of the crews of *Blythe Spirit*, *One More Time*, *Breakin' Wind*, and *Ace*. *Blythe Spirit*, a Viking 28 moored to *Panache*'s port side and skippered by Steve and James, encapsulates the

Badlands spirit with raucous and barefooted energy. Because Mark had crewed with them for two years before buying his boat, their attitude toward *Panache* was akin to a big brother's treatment of an upstart younger sibling. Having nicknamed us *Panicky*, James took pleasure in pointing out our errors and exclaimed in horror if we overtook them on a downwind leg. I soon discovered they were mostly bark and little bite. During a race, I'd see up to eight, nine, ten people aboard their boat. Despite the party atmosphere they were famous for, despite their spartan boat, *Blythe*'s crew are competitive racers with extensive tactical knowledge. Only recently, years after the Badlands BBQs had ended and Steve and James had moved to another club, did the realization suddenly flash that *Blythe Spirit* is a bigger boat than *Panache*, with a hull two feet longer. Of course, a Viking 28 would be nearly impossible for a Niagara 26 to beat! Racing against them made us better, and I missed much more than their competitive spirit when they left.

I stared at my bank balance, calculating whether this was the year I could afford an associate membership at Queen City, even though I could still continue to crew on *Panache* without joining the club. It was only a couple of hundred dollars, but after resnt, minimum student loan and credit card payments, and bills, I rarely had that entire amount at one time. The constraints of my budget as a graduate student on scholarship, then as a tutor, writer, and ESL teacher, were stressful and tedious, but also freeing. There was a simplicity to my life when I was only thinking about writing, working, and when I would be paid. My embarrassment, isolation, and pride funnelled into a singleness of purpose. I knew this limbo state wouldn't last forever, even if it sometimes felt like it. I enjoyed my small pleasures—a thrift store jacket, a bag of overripe tomatoes for a dollar, and tender tickets that took me to the club for racing.

The cost of sailing can range from BBQ contributions and transportation to signing up for a dinghy class to buying a boat. Yacht clubs typically have different membership fee categories to suit how much time and money someone wants to invest into sailing. There are associate, social, or crewing memberships for people who don't own a boat, dry sail memberships for those who want to store a dinghy, and senior memberships for boat owners who pay for mooring, water and electricity, and storage lockers. There are dinghy clubs that operate on a co-operative model, where fees allow members to sign out a boat and join training and racing programs.

Fees can also vary widely from club to club, as each offers different amenities and attracts different demographics. Some clubs are more family-oriented while others are known for professional networking. Some have high initiation fees or "minimum billing," an amount a member is obligated to spend at club social events or in the dining room. Some may even have a wait-list to join and require a referral. Others have a large proportion of powerboaters, canoers, and kayakers. No matter which club you join, you are obliged to believe it to be the best and to find other clubs less favourable than your home club.

With every season, my sense of good fortune that I could sail so affordably and easily increased. Many clubs do not allow non-members to participate in their sailing programs, as Mark found when he was searching for a club to join. By allowing guests to crew who aren't members, Queen City lowers the financial barriers for people to participate in sailing, and in doing so, makes the club more attractive. This sense of welcome could be a deliberate strategy by board members to bring new faces to the club, especially as there are numerous clubs in the Toronto area for prospective members to consider. Like many other guests, I drifted idly through the grounds, unsure whether I would stay. But each season brought me back, and then I searched for a place to land, where I could draw nutrients from the warm air and fine filaments of friendship.

The Badlands is more than a place—it became an attitude. For those boats docked under the messy cottonwoods, the name is a reclamation of one of the least favourable areas of the club. Perhaps every club has an equivalent of the Badlands, where the younger generation of serious racers congregates. Taking turns barbecuing was cheaper and more fun than eating at the club restaurant. The skippers and crews of *Ace*, *Blythe Spirit*, *Breakin' Wind*, and *Panache* would also frequently meet during the off-season for "dry land training" sessions, which I mistakenly used to believe involved actual training rather than keeping one's liver in active condition in the winter. The ever-cheerful Jeannette, who, along with her husband, Dave, owned *Breakin' Wind*, a C&C 27, contributed much of the energy behind the Badlands' social activity. At the end of the season, Jeannette used the funds from returned beer cans to install a can crusher and to order QCYC *The Badlands*–branded ball caps. I only wear mine on special occasions.

Even though we were racing against each other, skippers frequently traded crew members. The substantial friendships were like invisible towing lines linking the boats. Even on the fringes of this group, I felt the care—the offers of spare parts or a tow, the advice over boat maintenance and racing tactics, the hours spent listening to each other's life updates. On blue-bottle summer evenings, we stood around picnic tables, saying we were going leave on the next tender back to the city but delaying our departure by another half-hour, and then another. We complained there were more and more people to feed, as other members hungry for dinner and for post-race gossip were drawn into the buzz, but there was always enough to go around. I listened in as Jess and Dan recounted winter offshore races, as James embellished sly tactics, or when Jeff and Meghan from *Ace* offhandedly told me stories of injuries and close calls.

Mentally, I stood at the edge of the circle. I wasn't ready for sailing to be a bigger part of my life, but nonetheless I absorbed the ethos of the Badlands—not complaining if my pants were soaked through with lake spray, getting up at 7:00 a.m. for a regatta after availing myself of the free rum pours the night before, having more fun losing in a close race than winning consistently in a fleet that failed to offer lively competition. I thought all sailors shared these attitudes. I didn't know any better, and when I did, it was too late. I was already surrounded by the Badlands atmosphere, and I didn't want to be elsewhere.

I've heard the term *cliquishness* applied to friendships in the sailing communities, with connotations of exclusivity and high school. I didn't have the years of racing experience that other people in the Badlands had, and I was startled by the amount of time they'd invested in it since they were teen-agers. It's a subdued kind of privilege to be able to grow up sailing. The choice to become more involved in sailing is also a privilege. I saw so many possible paths before me. I could step forward into a space I was already welcome in, thanks to my crewing on *Panache*, a space that may have been formed in reaction to the older and more conservative elements of the club. When cliques come into existence, they also bring to attention the conditions that necessitated their formation. Those on the edge of the community also have a role. Their involvement and presence form a permeable boundary—they are the boundary.

Something about the word *community* and its use has always bothered me, possibly because it has become pervasive in the discourse of political leaders, media, organizations, and insti-tutions that use phrases like "diverse communities" and "cre-ative communities." The concept of community in those con-texts feels contrived in an attempt to speak to and on behalf of everyone. The word is used to evoke a sense of solidarity, belonging, and inclusivity that isn't present, that collapses differences such as ethnicity, culture, gender, class, and other identities.

When I first started to publish and to participate in Toronto's literary events, the spaces were male-dominated, lacking in diversity, overly reliant on volunteer labour, and rife with avoidant behaviours, addiction, and abuses of power. I craved a supportive circle of writers, and several times I felt I'd almost found it among writers who poured their time and energy into hosting readings, editing magazines, and publishing chapbooks. Yet despite their efforts, shifts were incrementally slow. Standing outside a bar with a coterie of male editors and writers, I told myself that these were my friends, my supporters, and my allies. But I felt an active sublimation of identity—there were things I never brought up and stories I didn't tell.

I was able to find a community of writers of colour by creating it myself. In our gatherings, I was nourished by their presences, and by conversations that felt powerful and urgent. We shared good news and stories that elicited nods, sighs, and head-shakes. I also witnessed conflicts and challenges. Even though we were all racialized writers, we didn't have the same experiences, access, or privilege. Many good things came from our conversations, such as a conference for writers of colour, anthologies, and being asked to give workshops on equity and diversity. For years afterwards, I kept being asked whether I would organize these gatherings again. While the sharing and the relationships were substantial, it required a ton of volunteer labour and proliferated tasks and projects. This kind of community-building didn't feel like a natural or spontaneous process. I had hoped that it would proliferate itself without so much continual effort and consciousness on my part, like sowing seedlings in hospitable soil.

My parents' stories of growing up in Hong Kong gave me pictures of the closely knit circles of neighbours and family that I had never known. My father's family were among the educated and wealthy business owners who fled Shanghai after the communists gained power, and he spent hours bored at the mah-jong parties between my Nai-Nai and other

Shanghainese wives. My mother, from one of Hong Kong's islands, Peng Chau, was constantly watched by relations and villagers who scolded her rebellious temper, her miniskirts, her habits of reading and playing records too loudly.

Though they don't use the word *community*, my parents' relationships and experiences in Hong Kong exemplify a dichotomous concept that Ferdinand Tönnies published in 1887. The German sociologist defined the terms "community," or Gemeinschaft, and "society" or "association," Gesellschaft. He used Gemeinschaft to refer to groups that have a feeling of togetherness. Their relationships are organic, lasting, and authentic, such as those between families or a village. Those in the group act not out of personal interest but to benefit everyone. Their values are associated with folk cultures and customs, and because of their ties to tradition, tend toward conservatism. Communities maintain their equilibrium through emphasizing conformity and morality, excluding those who threaten their implicit social code.

In direct opposition, Gesellschaft refers to associations or groups in society that form when people share a common rational goal. These relations are calculated, commercial, self-interested, and temporary. Balance is maintained through policing and the justice system, and these rules are explicit. This category includes things like professional associations and unions, perhaps even cities and towns. I find these categorizations to be simplistic, but Gemeinschaft and Gesellschaft were meant to be tools for conceptualizing social relations and not literal categories. A pervasive concept in community studies is that the idea of community is under continual threat by urbanization, industrialization, market capitalism, and globalization. Tönnies's idealized concept of community is invoked as a means to critique urban industrialized societies, especially by those who call for the reclamation of a sense of an altruistic community amid the alienating and artificial relations of the city or corporation.

In spite of Toronto's energy, I can't deny that living in Canada's largest city can be cold and isolating. I have made friends and colleagues, but there's a sense of distance, of not wanting to impose, a hecticness to our lives that undoes attempts at intimacy. In contrast, my mom tells me of how everyone knew everyone in her village, how safe it was for children to wander around alone. But she also speaks about how strong the pressure was to conform and to be a dutiful daughter. She appreciates the freedom she has in Canada, whereas I find satisfaction in being under obligation to others. I wonder if the two categories, the traditional community and the constructed one, can coexist.

Each side of my family occupied a different social status, and so my relationship with class and privilege is a complex one. On the Shanghainese side, my great-grandfather worked on the grounds of a Dutch missionary, and so my Yei-Yei, father, and aunt attended Catholic school. My grandfather attended and taught at a university, and was a factory owner before he took his family to Hong Kong. My aunt studied in Canada, where she may have belonged to a sorority. On the Cantonese side, my Gong-Gong was also educated, having passed his Chinese civil service exam, but in the tumult of the Japanese invasion during the Second World War, he was never able to take up a government position. On the island, my enterprising Poh-Poh started a dry-goods store that supported the entire extended family. In Canada, one of my uncles was employed at a golf club in Vaughan, while another managed one of U of T's college cafeterias. They've done well—becoming property owners, going on frequent vacations, and putting my cousins through university and graduate school. When I hear the argument that Hong Kong people benefited from colonialism, I can't deny that this is partially true for my family. They escaped the hardships of the Chinese revolution, learned English, and were able to emigrate to Canada. But their lives were not free of suffering, struggle, or a sense of exile.

I carry all of this history wherever I go. When I visit yacht clubs, the thought at the back of my mind is how they are spaces that have historically excluded people like my family, especially in colonial Hong Kong. Only British naval officers were permitted to join the Royal Hong Kong Yacht Club, founded in 1894, and Chinese people were not allowed membership until the 1950s. My Shanghainese grandparents would've approved of my participation in any exclusive or elite club or organization. Many Chinese have similar attitudes toward Ivy League colleges, sports such as cricket, horseback riding, and golf, and luxury brands. Yet the waiter who mixed me a Caesar at a regatta party reminded me of my uncles. I couldn't see myself as a member of a yacht club but felt strangely guilty as I continued to use and enjoy the club's amenities without paying for them. One year I asked the membership chair if he thought I should join, and I was grateful that he didn't put any pressure on me. He reminded me that the club benefited when I bought tender tickets, ate at the club restaurant, and brought friends to crew and to visit. Belonging is more than membership.

Queen City's membership fees are lower than those of most clubs around Toronto, but with the caveat that members are required to contribute to its "self-help" ethic. The club hires a minimum of staff for maintenance, facilities, and the office, and everything else is done by the volunteer labour of members. Senior members are nominated and elected each year to chair areas such as entertainment, communications, membership, racing programs, clubhouse and grounds maintenance, the yard, moorings, and so on. For years I watched Mark pour in hundreds of volunteer hours, many more than his obligated minimum. He has acted as webmaster for the QCYC website, as chair of the Open Regatta, and as house chair responsible for coordinating clubhouse maintenance, repairs, and the restaurant and bar operations. When I first learned about the work-hours program, I felt even more unmotivated to join—why would anyone pay to do free labour? That a community's sense of belonging would be contingent on paying fees and mandated working hours felt like an artificial construct at best, and possibly exploitative at worst.

At Queen City, there's a sense of welcome, care, and relationality that I recognize, but I can't recall where I've known it before. There's a throwback feel to social activities such as a pig roast, Sailpast, banquets, trivia nights, raffles, fundraisers, potlucks, movie nights on the lawn. The club's socializing is intentionally staged through the unironic cover bands that play old standbys, the donning of blue and white for Sailpast, and the display of club trophies and vintage photographs. This creates a contrast between the club's sense of tradition and that of Toronto's constant construction and reinventions—yet communities themselves are constructed things. The club's atmosphere simultaneously places itself outside of trends even as it reacts to them. It's nostalgic even as it continues to beget nostalgia.

Traditionally, Chinese society valued the needs of the collective over those of the individual. In the wake of the war and revolution, my grandparents' generation set aside things like personal comfort for the sake of housing, food, and basic survival. However, my parents find these traditional values to be patriarchal and narrow-minded. My dad struggled with the strict British school system and was a source of shame for his parents, even though he likely had a learning disability. My Nai-Nai was disappointed and angry that her only son, for whom she had sacrificed so much, emigrated to Canada at twenty-three rather than staying to fulfill his filial duty. My mom adored school and inherited her father's talent for literature and calligraphy. But because she was a girl, she was sent to earn her own living in Hong Kong garment factories, for which she still hasn't quite forgiven my grandmother. Going against typical Chinese parental behaviour, my parents told my sister and me endless stories and encouraged us to draw, paint, play music, and imagine.

As the daughter of non-conformists, of artists, and of immigrants, I identify strongly with being an outsider. Even when I do have a claim to citizenship, membership, and ownership, I often feel like a guest. When I began sailing, I didn't see many others at the club who shared my background. The people I met gave me the impression that they hadn't had to constantly prove their identity, their fluency in English, and their Canadian-ness in the same way I had. I saw how club members valued QCYC history and praised members who served the community. Even though I clapped during awards banquets, I felt I was listening to a history that wasn't mine.

But I didn't share my history with them either, not even those in the Badlands. What I had seen of the club hadn't convinced me that the community was invested in social change. I took it for granted that they wouldn't understand my beliefs and values. I didn't want to burden others with my fraught views of class and colonialism. I showed up on Wednesday nights, raced with my crew, ate dinner, and took the tender home. Being an outsider feels safe and free from the burden of responsibility. An outsider does not need to benefit the community or to conform. Yet this position comes from defensive deficit thinking. It deprived me of deepening relationships that could have given me a greater sense of belonging.

Lineage is important in sailing. I was fortunate to race with a skipper with a strong sense of fairness, who valued safety and who didn't take racing so seriously that he forgot we were supposed to be having fun. Listening to Mark and other experienced racers, I ingested the values of good sportsmanship. The "golden rule" of sailing, derived from the *Racing Rules of Sailing*, was to avoid collision. This rule also means not being a danger to oneself and others, racing in your proper fleet, and racing the correct course. It means not barging the start line or calling for mark room when there is no overlap, rounding marks properly even if there are no boats around to witness it, and doing penalty turns with good grace. Mark was vocal in complaints when other skippers and crew didn't display the same respect for the rules. He'd repeat the story of their behaviour to anyone hanging around the Badlands, airing his grievances and confirming that the other boat was in the wrong, and listening to others' perspectives. Seeing and hearing experienced racers' reactions to each other's stories had an influence on newer crew, and sociologists might see this as part of a socialization process. Years later, I found myself being an agent of socialization for those new to racing, repeating and acting out what had been shown to me. It was a strange feeling, like hearing someone else's voice come out of my mouth.

The conceptualization of community that I feel most aligned to is that of Welsh cultural critic Raymond Williams, who, like me, finds its positive associations "suspicious." In his 1977 essay "The Importance of Community," he describes growing up in a small rural community and living among neighbours who had habits of "mutual obligation," but he's careful not to idealize these habits. Instead, Williams emphasizes that this "level of social obligation" that arose from people living in the same region and having a "common identity" could generate "acts of kindness beyond calculation" and "forms of mutual recognition." I have both seen and received countless ungrudging acts of kindness at Queen City, ranging from the simple, such as help transporting items to the club or the loan of a rudder when *Panache*'s was broken, to meaningful acts of care such as hospital visits when a club member was ill. The commonality of sailing and club membership feels like a pretext for friendship and community, where the self-help ethic and the sense of obligation it induces opens the gates for a much more significant feeling of responsibility and relationality.

Williams suggests that community may not find that it can depend on this relative sense of stability and custom, and it needs tensions and fierce conflict to hammer out more positive outcomes. What I find most valuable about Williams's analysis is the demystification of the ideal of a traditional community, which can be nostalgized and used as a political appeal to create a sense of absolute obligation. Describing community as the sphere of "direct and directly responsible relationships" neither represents community as wholly positive nor necessarily toxic, but as complex and reciprocal. It's a vision of community as a constant negotiation of those relations. It emphasizes compromise, mutual comprehension, and relationship-building over the static values of its members. Williams's ideas have many resonances not only in the sailing community but in any social sphere defined by its relations.

What yacht clubs offer in return for numerous fees and responsibilities is a pretext for acts of kindness and mutual obligation. As a result, they can be refuges from large, impersonal cities and ideal places for newcomers to find community. Anti-social members who pay their fees but who never pitch in don't get as much from the club as they might otherwise. A good member of the sailing community is someone who gets to know others and lets others know them. The most highly praised and popular members are those who are active as racers, as cruisers, as volunteers, or all three. I asked Bruce

Smith, the club's elected rear commodore and responsible for organizing the club's racing programs, why it felt like it was always the same few names who were always helping out at Queen City. Sighing, Bruce reminded me of the 80/20 rule, which he also found to be true at other clubs around the lake. It's inevitable, he said, that 20 percent of any community are doing 80 percent of the work. I vowed to myself I wouldn't join until I was sure I could contribute to the club in a sub-stantial way. But I wasn't sure how to quantify a substantial contribution. Even though the number of volunteer hours aren't onerous, I felt that someone with my tendencies would be easily sucked into doing much more.

The Badlands post-race BBQs dispersed after a few seasons, when James and Steve moved *Blythe Spirit* to the Ashbridge's Bay Yacht Club, when others sustained damage to their boats and no longer raced, or when they started families and had less time for socializing at the club. The current carried away our friends to new adventures. *Breakin' Wind*, *Ace*, and *Blythe Spirit* were replaced at their Badlands slips with boats that didn't race and owners we hardly saw. The picnic area grew weedy and the mini-fridge underneath the cottonwoods remained vacant. At first, busy with my own life, I hardly noticed this slow fading of faces. Then their absences felt sudden and acute, like a gap in the canopy when a hearty, blooming tree has been chopped down.

When I looked deeper into the Queen City history and archives, I saw evidence of constant changes, upgrades, renovations, and revisionings. Some events exist only in the memories of club members, making it hard to pin down dates and origin stories. I suspect that many of the club's traditions began as one-off gatherings and parties, or as the brainchild of a few quixotic members. They might've gone unrecorded except as a brief mention in a club newsletter or a photograph in a box in the back of a storage locker. They might've faded from view, only to be revitalized again years later. Club historians such as Richard Slee and the late Wayne Lilley have had to piece together events from conversations, club meeting agendas, and other scraps into a shared story.

Historically, sailing clubs have been geared toward people of a certain class—of a privileged, white, and male demographic. But they are also fluid entities that shift with each new addition to the membership roster. I presume that they may be slower to incorporate feminist, intersectional, and decolonial perspectives, but I haven't been privy to the leadership's past decision-making. Nor is it fair of me to make generalizations about the membership of a club such as Queen City, which I know includes people deeply committed to social justice, activism, and progressive politics. The reliance on volunteer labour and constantly changing membership may make it difficult to maintain momentum in doing equity, diversity, and inclusivity work. Yet the way that sailing communities have the potential to bring together diverse perspectives is one of their strengths. The club leadership and board change each year, and this turnover is necessary for the sustainability of the community, as it imbues the club with new ideas and voices.

With each season, I gain more insight into how the club community functions. Sailors are practical people, jettisoning rules, practices, and programs that no longer serve them.

Therefore, the status quo is maintained only insofar as it serves the community, and sailors are open to changes if the changes are beneficial and, perhaps more importantly, if they have been consulted. There is always a danger of racist, sexist, and predatory individuals within any club or organization. There may always be members who take up sailing as an escape from discourse of political correctness and are less willing to view the community critically. But there are others who understand that tolerating outdated and exclusionary views or being passive to change could damage Queen City's reputation, detract from membership and the growth of the club. Ultimately, that is not what the club spirit is about. I hadn't realized that, even before I became a member, my presence and participation at the club was part of a greater transformation.

I've always hoped that another Badlands era might begin, but in the past several seasons I've seen something taking place at the club that is more widespread and inclusive. Fresh-faced crews have become the new generation of racers. Daughters who used to crew with their dads bought boats of their own, became senior members, and began contributing actively as board members. Former sailing instructors bought boats and raced with all-female crews. A group of guys in their late twenties, with no previous sailing experience, bought a C&C 27. A couple with two young kids bought a Tanzer 22 that was assigned the slip next to *Panache*, and I would often see them enjoying their boat on the weekends. These members had active Instagram accounts where they posted their adventures of sailing and swimming around Lake Ontario. It was hilarious to me that some of these newer members came to Mark for advice, just as he'd go to older members for their boat maintenance and racing wisdom. Ever generous with their time, long-time sailing champions Dan Smith and Jess Mace lead training sessions to improve the fleet's strategy and tactics, and they are constantly fielding requests to restart the sessions.

The pandemic had a detrimental effect on race participation, and only now are the numbers recovering. As a result, experienced crew are in high demand and find themselves jumping onto short-handed boats, myself included. This has created a stronger camaraderie between racers. Now, on Wednesday nights, tables are pushed together at the clubhouse. Across the lagoon, I see the lights as crews mix and socialize. On one Monday-night dinghy race, I crewed with Rachel, a past sailing instructor. As we finished the race, she told me about an under-forty chat group that had organized a DJ dance party on the *Rapids Queen* that acts as a breakwater in front of the club. "But I'm over forty," I said, laughing, and she said it didn't matter. I didn't feel left out—it's important that the younger members have a space to call their own. It gladdens me that the Badlands spirit has seeded itself around the club. We had never tried to keep it to ourselves, and it would've been impossible to try.

Knowing When to Quit

"IS THAT OUR COURSE?" I ask, pointing toward the bobbing committee boat.

"No," Mark calls over the rumble of the outboard motor. "We're further out."

Quentin, Jay, Perry, Astra, and I gaze at the boats hovering near their start line, some with both sails hoisted, some with only their mains, others still motoring. Mark steers past them, and we continue to scan the hoop of the horizon. Faintly, a few miles out, we see another group of tiny white triangles. Lake Ontario curls around them, its slate-blue water scrawled with faint foam and teases of sunlight. The lake takes my attention and spreads it wide. Behind us, the island's beaches and shoreline of elm and oak retreats. The panorama of Toronto's skyline stretches and fades to Burlington and Hamilton. Here and there, marker and weather buoys are pinned to the waves: a big painted drum, a yellow stick, a pillar, a red or green beacon. The triangles get bigger, growing from kerchiefs to blankets. Mark shuts off the motor far enough from the committee boat that we can hoist the sails without running into the other competitors. Then we check in, gauge the length of the start line, wait for our starting sequence. I took for granted that we'd find the racecourse. I took for granted that we'd arrive on time. There are many things I assume are the skipper's responsibility, things I don't even know how to be responsible for. I can sense that there's much more to this business of racing sailboats than meets the eye. The sensation is like picking a film out of a bargain bin and getting that gut twinge that you'll never be the same after watching what it has to offer you.

Here's what I knew about regattas in my first few years: that they were all-day or multi-day races organized by a racing council or association, that they were hosted by a participating member club. Unlike our short weeknight races in the harbour, we needed to catch an early tender and motor out of the lagoon in time for our start. I knew that regatta courses had legs of nearly a mile, and that with enough wind there could be three or four races each day. The downwind legs were long enough to make hoisting and flying the spinnaker worthwhile. Mark had entered his boat into the flying sails fleet for each of the Lake Ontario Racing Circuit (LORC) weekend regattas throughout the summer, which I knew would keep us extremely busy on the foredeck. I knew enough to follow instructions and not be too much of a liability on board. There was much, much more that I and the rest of crew didn't know, though. Our lack of knowledge filled an empty shelf. Even with his experience, Mark was still learning how to optimize the boat's speed and to point higher into the wind. The rest of us barely understood how to handle the boat in overpowering conditions, and we couldn't tell when the boat was being lifted and headed in wind shifts. But ignorance can serve a purpose—in our case, it prevented us from worrying about things we didn't need to worry about. Ignorance protected us.

As autumn approaches Southern Ontario, the wind becomes livelier and whitecaps break across the bow. Did I know it was possible to get seasick on the lake? I'm rarely afflicted by motion sickness, so before my first regatta in late September 2009, I wasn't suspicious of the lake's swell and buckle. The regatta, co-hosted by National and Queen City that year, was the last of the season. The day brought flushes to our skin, the sun was a bright coin, and the wind gusty. Since I'd gotten on the water, my stomach had felt like someone was poking and kneading it, and my queasiness increased halfway to the windward mark. The bright scissors of light, the bow sinking into the trenches of the waves, and the uninterrupted expanse of the lake should've been a delight, but instead they were scrambling my inner signals. I felt thwarted by my body, and an acid frustration rose in my throat. In the lull between the first race and the second, I climbed down into the cabin, found a plastic bag, and quietly heaved into it. I rose out of the cabin and took my seat on the high side and said nothing, swallowing more than just fresh air.

Among our mishaps that day were an over-early start, an uphaul clipped on over the jib sheets, and changing to a smaller headsail on the downwind only to realize that the wind had shifted, which put us behind and off course. We were also sailing with a borrowed spinnaker pole, as a few days earlier *Panache*'s spinnaker pole-end had broken off and tumbled into the lake. The crew had been using the spinnaker pole in place of the whisker pole, which had broken twice. Whisker and spinnaker poles are durable but not indestructible pieces of equipment, and to break both poles within a single season implied some misuse.

Nonetheless, as Mark recounted on his blog, *Panache* finished the two-day regatta first overall, earning a new yellow flag. Only two boats had raced in our flying sails division, the other a similarly sized Beneteau named *Shimakaze*. We observed *Shimakaze* gaining on us or forcing us to tack under them at the start, but they too seemed to struggle to sheet in sails in the unkempt wind. I was too busy trying not to heave my breakfast across the bow and with resetting spinnaker lines to pay much attention to the competition, so our performance was a surprise to me. I tended to tally up our mistakes rather than to recognize what we'd done well, such as communicating effectively and recovering quickly. This kind of uneven accounting is itself a mark of inexperience.

For a daylong regatta I now pack boat shoes, a rain jacket, beer, lunch and snacks, sunscreen, a hat, sunglasses with a lanyard, rain pants, a full change of clothes that includes socks and underwear, and, depending on the time of year, a toque, scarf, and gloves. On gusty days, the lake reaches its wet fingers over the high side of the boat, soaking my legs. A light rain will slick the foredeck and soak through the seat of my pants as I sit on the bow. Because I mind being soaked less than my crew, I will turn and block a crashing wave from splashing the others sitting along the rail—so noble of me. Afterwards, I have dripped and squished into the washroom at the club and stripped off layers. I have run my fingers under hot water, waiting for the chill to exit them. I have crawled into bed sunburned, with a touch of sunstroke, slight flares behind my eyelids. I have lain on my mattress feeling as though it were tipping from side to side. And yet each season I sign myself up for more, as if these short stints of discomfort are a reminder of how free of suffering my life really is.

Thinking I might be lost, I'd walked the winding driveway leading to Port Credit Yacht Club until I glimpsed the tops of the masts waving beside the pine and fir trees at Lakefront Promenade Park, the boats protected by a long, rocky breakwater. I curiously circled the grounds, feeling like an intruder, but I received nods and smiles in the corridors when I paused to look at club trophies, kind directions to the washrooms, and attentive service from the servers who were overwhelmed by the influx of sailors in need of lubrication. When throwing a LORC regatta party, the hosting club puts on their best face. They plan ahead by securing rum sponsors, hiring a local band to sing Neil Diamond covers, and corralling volunteers for barbecuing duty. Later on, *Panache*'s crew not only compared how we did against other boats in our division, but also contrasted the regatta organization, the number of beer tickets handed out, the food, the friendliness, and the atmosphere with that of our own club.

On my visits to other clubs, I noted that National Yacht Club has the advantages of a downtown location, proximity to the Billy Bishop Airport, and a wide porch around a handsome square clubhouse, but its grounds are limited. It can be tricky to spot Ashbridge's Bay Yacht Club from behind the curved spit, but it's worth a visit for its family-friendly environment, veranda, and gazebo. The many-columned clubhouse at Royal Canadian Yacht Club, near Centre Island, is surrounded by lawn bowling and tennis courts. Uniformed staff glide under gleaming candelabras in the banquet hall.

I compared each club's conveniences and assets: a wall of windows wrapping around an elegant dining room; kayaks, paddleboards, and bikes for members to sign out; washrooms stocked with shampoo and lotion; a water taxi to fetch sailors docked at swing moorings; complimentary parking. I watched people my age carry pitchers to their tables, listened to an older skipper recount his reasons for retiring early from the race, and let my gaze settle on a group of women wearing matching neon green jerseys. When visiting other clubs, I admired their amenities and atmosphere but invariably felt like something was missing. I was glad, nonetheless, for a different set of views that reminded me of what my own club lacked and what it offered.

Between the months of May and October, Lake Ontario is criss-crossed with racing activity. There are one-design regattas, long-distance races, short-handed races, women's skipper regattas, able sail events, and Canadian and North American one-design championships. These events include open regattas, where any boat from participating clubs can register, or invitationals, where competitors can be limited or restricted to a particular club or boat design. These events aren't broadcast on sporting channels and aren't recorded, which has always felt like a shame to me. There's enough drama, dialogue, and thrills for hours of riveting viewing, and, in my opinion, they're much more entertaining than a hockey or football game.

These races and regattas accommodate a range of skill and competition levels and include the LORC Open Regattas, the Lake Ontario Short Handed Race Series, organized by Lake Ontario Offshore Racing, and the overnight Susan Hood Trophy Race and Lake 300/600 Challenge Races. The Lake Yacht Racing Association, founded in 1884, hosts a multi-day event in July out of Kingston Yacht Club. The Golden Horseshoe Yacht Racing Association hosts a five-day regatta the first week of July, with multiple races between Burlington, Bronte Harbour, Hamilton, Dalhousie, Newport, and Port Credit yacht clubs. If that's not enough sailing for one week, competitors can also race the FIASCO Regatta earlier in the weekend, a long-distance pursuit race of twenty-two nautical miles, also held in the Golden Horseshoe region of western Lake Ontario. Inspired by the Three Bridge Fiasco race in San Francisco, this race has three simultaneous start and finish lines so that participants can race without having to motor long distances from their home ports. The Race to Kingston kicks off at Mimico Cruising Club at Toronto's western edge and ends in Kingston Harbour. A hard-core group of racers at the Harbour City Yacht Club in Toronto Island Marina began a club Frostbite Series in the 1970s, a series of weekend races that made the most of warm fall weather before haulout. Other clubs were interested in joining, so the AHMEN series was begun. The name is an acronym of the founding clubs:

Alexandra, Harbour City, Mimico, Etobicoke, and National. Participants from other clubs in the area race as well since there are no registration fees. "AH-MEN!" is the quiet thanks we give our boat after completing the single day's race around a number of difficult-to-spot buoys, painted drums, and sticks that make up the racecourse.

For more casual racers like *Panache*'s crew, spending a day racing the AHMEN or LORC series is a step up in intensity from our weeknight club races. There are multiple races a day, flying sails, and competition from other clubs. Recreational sailors keen on racing can fill their calendar with regattas and long-distance races. The most competitive sailors can register for the CORK regattas, an international event hosted in the Portsmouth Olympic Harbour in Kingston. Serious racers can also invest in boats like Lasers, Stars, J22s, or other one-design models. When I peruse the racing calendars, I see events that could help me to expand into the sailor I have yet to become.

I can't give a bird's-eye view of *Panache*'s performance during a race or offer a play-by-play of every wind shift and overlap. On the foredeck, I have a limited view of my surroundings, of the course, our position, the competition. Craning or jumping for a better view disturbs the balance of the boat, and so I focus on things I can easily see, such as the sails, lines, halyards, the position of start and finish lines, marks, wind shifts, lulls, and gusts. Being focused while crewing means not knowing everything that is taking place on the racecourse.

My recounting of a race is in bits and pieces, and after several seasons, regattas have started to blend into each other. I remember brushing away dozens of tiny flies during an ABYC regatta in May while easing a spinnaker sheet and squinting up at the striped sail. I remember staggering under a spinnaker pole when Phil or Perry or Jay released the halyard too quickly. I remember my fingers being too cold to undo the shackle that attached the jib to the deck. I remember the wind shifting so much that we launched the chute on what was supposed to be an upwind leg—or was it the other way around? Did we, in fact, haul everything in on what was supposed to be a downwind finish? I remember having to dig deep for reserves of strength on the fourth race of the day, my arms aching as I once again hoisted, trimmed, and doused sails. The things that I can recall most clearly are moments of high panic and exhausted satisfaction. Isn't it strange that memory falls into these extremes? I reach for the in-between, uncountable moments of climbing with heavy breaths onto the windward side as the boat sped on a long upwind leg, gaining on the boat ahead or being gained upon by the boat behind.

This is a list of the mishaps, fouls, and breakages Mark noted on his blog that took place during *Panache*'s first season of racing regattas in 2009:

- a stanchion snapping off its base (likely because of a heavy object falling on it, such as a 180-pound crew member),
- a crew member letting off the spinnaker halyard instead of the jib halyard and letting drop a sail he'd just been raising a few moments before,
- the pin falling out of the snap shackle on the end of one of the spinnaker sheets so that it needed to be tied on for subsequent races,

- a new crew member becoming tangled in the jib sheets,
- running out of gas as the boat entered the lagoon, and
- the outboard motor rattling when the throttle was too high and failing to push the boat faster than two knots.

The following took place over the two days of the ABYC Open one late September:

- one crew member being gashed across his stomach on the first day of the regatta when attempting to catch a roll of sail tape tossed to us by the crew of *Blythe Spirit* (fortunately, we had a crew member on board who'd completed medical school),
- tearing a hole in the spinnaker during a douse that required patching with the aforementioned sail tape,
- the carabiner that attached the jib sheet to the lead car came apart during the first race, but thanks to a previous conversation with James on *Blythe Spirit* about the weak ability of carabiners, Mark had a few stainless-steel shackles on hand,
- the lone foredeck crew member having difficulty managing the spinnaker pole on his own and setting it up upside-down and twisted, resulting in a tricky gybe and falling behind the fleet,
- attempting to fly the spinnaker in fifteen to twenty knots of wind where the boat kept rounding up and flattening and requiring three crew members to gybe the pole,
- during the same race, the crew neglected to secure the spinnaker halyard after the douse so that it was streaming too high to be reached,
- spending several minutes trying to raise a backup spin halyard, an old and crusted line that didn't want to

budge, and so, unsurprisingly, once it was raised it didn't want to come back down again,

- two crew members nearly tumbling in the lake in high winds, saved only by clutching the mast or grabbing a shroud, and by the end of the day all the crew were bruised and exhausted, and
- sailing hungover in day two of the regatta after the previous night's party with liberal free-pours of rum and one too many Dark 'n' Stormy pitchers.

The more seasons I sailed, the more questions I had. How did Mark decide which end of the start line to cross? How was he able to decide whether to start on a port tack or a starboard one? How did skippers choose between tacking up the centre of the course or going out further? Why was it that, with such a large racing area, boats crossed each other so closely on opposite tacks, sometimes needing to bear off to duck the other? How was it that two or three boats beating upwind on different tacks end up at the windward mark at nearly the same time? Sometimes I asked these questions, sometimes I didn't, not always knowing if they were the right kinds of questions to ask. I had grasped the basics of racing, and now I was overwhelmed with the many exceptions, complications, and variations.

"When you knew less, you were more confident," Mark said recently as I despaired over remembering what the ticklers were telling me about the wind flow on the windward and leeward sides of the jib sail. "You know so much more now, and you're less sure of yourself."

A parade of sailboats with their spinnakers flying is a majestic sight—the triangular sails balloon like silken canopies. From a distance they appear to glide before the wind, giving no indication of the crew's scrambling exertions to keep the sail from collapsing in light air or to gybe it through wind shifts. Such a large sail, nearly twice the size of the main, is an unwieldy, wayward thing. It's typically made of nylon for its strength, flexibility, and weight. The chute is only used on downwind legs to catch the wind like a net. For clubs that race on the lake, it's typical to race with the spinnaker, but the racecourses in the harbour are too short to make putting up flying sails worthwhile.

When unused, *Panache*'s striped fuchsia, blue, and white spinnaker is packed into a grey bag called a turtle. On each of its three corners is a metal ring, and the ring at the head and the two bottom corners, or clews, should be stacked together before the sail is stuffed into the bag. On the foredeck, Quentin and I hook the bag up to the bow pulpit rail and then attach the halyard and sheets, running them outside everything on the boat and through blocks at either end of the stern. Before we head out, Mark retrieves the spinnaker pole from the rack in the boatyard. *Panache*'s spinnaker pole is customized to the size of the boat, around three inches in diameter and over ten feet in length, and has end fittings that resemble closed claws that can be opened with a trip mechanism. It's more awkward than heavy. I feel like a jouster when I tuck the pole under my arm, except instead of a horse I'm riding a buckling foredeck, and instead of trying to unseat my opponent I'm attempting to hook its end to a slippery ring. Back when I started racing, I knew the *what* and *how* of flying the spinnaker but not the *why*. As in: Why bother with it? Why is it worth the trouble?

Here is what should happen and how: As we approach the upwind mark, Quentin and I prepare by lifting the pole from where it lies along the deck, and I attach it to the mast, jaws turned up, and unhook the uphaul, closing its shackle around the ring that dangles from the centre of the pole, attached by two wires. It's important to not twist these wires. At the outboard end, Quentin attaches the sheets and lines to the spinnaker and the pole, then readies the sail by pulling it slightly out of its bag. After we have rounded the mark, the other crew hoist the spinnaker. All is well if it balloons immediately. The crew then adjusts the position of the pole with the uphaul and the spinnaker sheets. As soon as the spinnaker is flying, the jib must come down, and as we yank it onto the deck in messy folds, the main is eased until the boom is nearly perpendicular to the boat. While Quentin pushes and holds the boom out, I'll scramble back to grab the other spinnaker sheet if there aren't enough hands. We stare up at the edges of billowing fabric, watching for wind shifts that are legible in the way the sail curls and snaps back out. *Panache* coasts on the downwind leg aided by the enormous surface area of the chute. When it goes smoothly, this cumbersome manoeuvre can feel like the parts of a machine working together. When it goes awry, it's important not to let anxiety fray you the next time, and the next. We're always adding to our mental to-do list—untwist lines, double-check shackles. More to remember means more to forget.

Then there was the time during one regatta when Quentin commented that jib looked "pretty baggy." Hearing about the episode from Mark and reading about it on his blog, I can hear Quentin's half-laugh even though I wasn't there. The forestay, a heavy gauge wire that runs from the bow to the top of the mast and keeps it from falling backwards, had come loose from the mast. The shrouds on port and starboard are also the pieces of standing rigging that help keep the mast up. In my mind's eye I envision the mast leaning backwards into the cockpit and crashing in a mess of lines and sails atop of the crew. Paul Horne saved the day by instructing the crew to attach the uphaul to the bow so that it could act as a de-facto stay, and they abandoned the race and motored home immediately to the club's mast crane. It was then that Mark noted that the small pin that holds the larger pin that attaches the forestay to the top of the mast was missing.

I tell this anecdote often because, like all sailing stories, there are so many lessons contained in it. How the breakage of such a small part can cause a domino-like effect. How valuable it is to have someone with decades of sailing experience on board to advise and reassure a less experienced crew. How there's no shame in abandoning a race when it's safer to quit than to continue. This is the kind of story that is just frightening enough to serve as an illustration of sailing's risks but not so terrifying that it scare people away from climbing aboard. It's a story useful for determining one's own threshold for danger.

I come across a diagram in an old Royal Yachting Association sailing manual that enables me to visualize a racecourse. It is a simple square grid, turned forty-five degrees so that the grid lines make a diamond shape. At the bottom of the diamond is the boat's starting position. If the boat's path follows the zigzagging diagonal grid lines, there are numerous possibilities up the middle of the course to the windward mark at the top. Imagining this grid onto an expanse of water ahead orients me to the invisible reference points that other skippers seem aware of. It's a map that I'm still learning to read, with its topography of apparent wind.

For instance, a boat could sail up the centre of the course, tacking often. This is the most direct route but can be slower because of the speed lost when turning the boat. It's a good path if the wind appears to be steady down the centre of the course and the crew are quick enough to execute fast tacks. If the wind favours one side of the course, another option is to choose either a port or starboard tack at the start, based on observation and luck, and to tack only when the boat is being lifted. This option might necessitate attempting to pull away from boats on the same tack to avoid getting stuck in their bad air. Yet another option is to play the odds and commit to one outer edge of the course grid where you think there is more wind, and to sail all the way out, going for speed and clean air before tacking once onto the layline. This is the imaginary path that extends from the mark at the highest possible angle that a boat could tack or gybe to clear it. If you lay the mark correctly, no additional tacks or gybes are required. Sailing the outside edge of the course is referred to as "banging the corners." It's a strategy that can be risky but is a viable choice if you have a boat that can point high and a skipper who can steer through the shifts. It's also an option if you have nothing to lose.

"Pointing higher" is a phrase I've heard so often while racing that at one point, I must have looked it up. When it seems like other people know something I should, I'm too shy to ask—that's what Google, Wikipedia, and countless sailing books, videos, and blogs are for. At first, I understood "pointing higher" to mean sailing at a higher angle upwind, so that a boat has fewer tacks to make toward the windward mark. In other words, a boat that isn't pointing well will have to sail a longer course.

Of course, this isn't the whole story. When a boat is close-hauled, it is sailing as close as possible to the no-go zone where it will stall. The closer the angle between the true wind direction and the boat's course, the higher it is pointing. But the problem is that as a boat turns into the wind it will lose speed and its heel. The jib sail will start to backwind or luff, which looks like a long bubble of air popping up along the forestay. This is known as "pinching." As it bears off, the boat will gain speed but move further away from the upwind mark. There is a slot known as the "groove," which is the ideal balance between direction and boat speed, the point of sail where you have a consistent angle of heel and can steer most efficiently. The boat feels like it's moving almost effortlessly, as if on the path of a well-designed life.

Picking the fastest path upwind is complicated by the fact that on a racecourse, every skipper is trying to do the same thing. A skipper not only considers the course and conditions such as wind, waves, and current but also what competing boats are doing. "It's always a game," Mark explains. "If we sail in the same conditions as the competition and we think we can sail more efficiently than them, then we should be able to beat them. If we have already lost time, for whatever reason, we may be more inclined to sail a different course, to roll the dice and hope for a lucky break."

A "lucky break" can mean either an increase of wind force or a slight shift in the wind direction from the bow of the boat to the stern, allowing for the boat to head up a few degrees and to sail closer to the mark. It can also mean a competing boat gets headed or knocked when the wind shifts toward the bow, so that the skipper should adjust their course and make additional tacks. Quite often, the crew of *Panache* has been surprised to find itself winning a race when a bigger, faster boat sails into a hole or is stuck in another boat's wind shadow, also known as bad air. It's important to know when to quit, but it's also important not to quit too soon—to stop trying after a discouraging start or when you're being overtaken by the rest of the fleet. Racing is as much about strategy and resilience as it is about the physical act of handling the boat. By not quitting or abandoning a race too early, we keep the game—and the possibility of winning—alive.

There are common themes in the errors and fouls that happened in *Panache*'s first few seasons on the racecourse. There are the minor mishaps like not remembering to secure sheets and halyards so that they dangled in the air or flew to the top of the mast. Being shorthanded can cause more serious accidents on board. Breakages result when the right sail isn't used in high winds, such as flying the spinnaker in twenty knots, and crew struggle to stay on board when attempting manoeuvres such as tacking and gybing. All these errors stem from a lack of practice and experience. It's no wonder we were nicknamed *Panicky*, thanks to the sight of our eager but inexperienced crew scrambling about the boat. Later, when we began winning flags, I chalked the continued use of this nickname up to envy of our crew's youth and energy. We could beat members with decades more experience than us because we were quicker, learning to recognize and prevent mistakes before they happened, and fixing issues without wasting time blaming ourselves or others. "I didn't see Panicky on the course at all," a skipper said to me recently. "Because *Panicky* didn't race," I said coldly. "*Panache* did." I politely refrained from mentioning that we had nearly lapped that skipper's boat. In sailing, like in life, being a gracious winner is as important as being a good loser.

For a long time, I agreed to every request. I agreed to write poetry reviews for $100 and allowed publications to post them online without additional pay. I agreed to serve on juries for grants and contests. I agreed to teach four or five ESL classes on rotation with a day's notice. I agreed to contract work that wasn't enough to cover rent, so that I still had to tutor in the evenings. I gave away my time for much less than it was worth. I was afraid the opportunities wouldn't come again if I refused or that I would appear ungrateful. No one was forcing me to be so productive and busy, but I had grown up hearing from my parents about immigrants having to work twice as hard to get ahead. I lost the ability to gauge how much was enough until my body started to reveal its exhaustion.

I began to notice that my white writer friends weren't being asked by emerging Asian-Canadian writers for feedback on their work, by racialized poets for book blurbs and reviews, or to speak on panels about equity and diversity in publishing. It was so hard to refuse this work that I saw as fulfilling and necessary, but I questioned how much of a role I wanted to have within a community and industry that required so much labour from writers of colour.

Looking back, I don't know if I would have done things differently. I hate to think that my pain and burnout were unavoidable, and the mantra of "no pain, no gain" frustrates me. Is the path toward success as a writer and toward greater diversity in writing and publishing necessarily a long, zigzagging one? What are people signing up for when they choose the path of a writer, if they desire better conditions and pay for their work, or more diverse stories and increased representation? When my workaholic habits did manifest a writing career, it seemed to justify the effort I had put in. Indeed, I continue to produce new work, edit, mentor, and volunteer at an intense pace, but the difference now is that I feel less guilt if I need to take a step back or withdraw altogether. I share this story with other writers frequently, and when I arrange the parts of it, I can see that there were other choices and courses open to me. I can see when a small but crucial part of myself was broken.

The only time I nearly refused my skipper's instruction was during the QCYC Open Regatta in 2013. The day was messy with rain and we were racing west of Toronto Islands in Humber Bay. I remember trying not to slip on the wet foredeck, and I doubted my ability to stay on board. On a downwind leg, I was standing in front of the mast, holding on to it as the spinnaker strained behind me like a giant, engorged belly. Somewhere nearby, Quentin was keeping me company, because we always needed two people when racing flying sails. The rest of the crew were tensed and hunched against the blowing rain, but no one was panicking. Their silent acceptance of the situation helped me to believe there was a semblance of normalcy in racing in such foul weather.

I remember that when Mark called out to us to gybe the spinnaker, a refusal rose up in my body. The feeling was so unfamiliar that I couldn't recognize it. I didn't want to let go of the mast to unhook the spinnaker pole, as I didn't think I could keep my footing on the slick foredeck. I tried to fight the fear, but still I hung on. I don't recall if Quentin and I carried out the manoeuvre. It must've been after that first race that Mark asked us if we were having fun, deciding to retire after the first race and motor home after seeing our weary faces. Or maybe I'm confusing it with another time. I can still feel my soaked socks and the dampness trickling down my neck.

Ten years later, I watched the full, unedited version of that regatta video, which had been filmed on Mark's GoPro. I saw us beating upwind in a steady eight to ten knots, all of us wearing bright jackets and hoods zipped tight up to our chins. Mark pushes back his hood for better visibility and the rain darkens his blond hair. I watch Pat holding the mainsheet and leaning to the side as Phil and Frankie crowd the cockpit to grind in the jib, and me and Quentin struggling to climb up to the high side. I see myself leaning back to say something to Mark, but I don't remember what I said, and afterwards I point to something in the distance. We follow *Blythe Spirit* upwind, but from what I can see, we are unable to overtake them.

The spinnaker bag is passed up to Quentin and he attaches it as the boat heels twenty degrees. The lake tosses up waves against the hull until the lines are soaked and heavy. Quentin and I crouch with the spinnaker pole attached to the mast and the clew end of the spinnaker. As we round the mark, Phil begins cranking up the spinnaker halyard as Frankie sheets in the starboard spin sheet until the pole begins to pull the kite out of the bag. Halfway up it begins to twist and fill. We douse the jib untidily onto the deck and we speed downwind. Mark must've told us to gybe the pole. I see my arm wrapped around the mast. With no sign of hesitation, Quentin and I manage to get the pole off the mast, but the boat gybes before we can get it across and the spinnaker twists. There's a moment of suspension as the boom gets caught in a sheet before Mark untangles it and the main flies across. As the boat flattens out, I see that Quentin and I have stowed away the pole.

We continue downwind, and on the foredeck we seem to be trying to untwist the spinnaker when a sudden gust heels the boat, and the mainsheet drags into the lake. Once again, the spinnaker sheet is caught on the boom, and it's only when Mark releases it that we can prepare to douse, which goes messily, the top of the sail dipping into the lake despite my best efforts to throw it into the cockpit as quickly as possible. I hear Mark's laughter as we head back upwind on our second lap and I am gesturing wildly with my arms after we've untangled the spinnaker sheets. The rest of the race is more of the same, but instead of dealing with the spinnaker again, we poled out the headsail, which gave us more than enough to power us to the finish line. The committee boat, *Freddy M*, was rocking like a cradle in the waves, and as the race committee sounded the horn for our finish, we were too tired to even cheer. I watch myself sitting motionless and stunned on the bow, my hands still gripping the lifelines.

"Good first race," Mark can be heard saying, which gets a few smiles. It had, at last, stopped raining. Was this the race where I'd been paralyzed at the mast, or was it another one? Or maybe what had felt like minutes of delay had only been, in reality, a few moments of trepidation, unnoticed by everyone around me.

Recently, my mother, looking at my Chinese horoscope, described me as "fearless." I protested. Like everyone, I feel afraid. She explained that she meant I have the ability to push through setbacks and failures and continue. And it was true, in a sense: rejection letters from publishers hadn't kept me from resubmitting, and my years of depression, burnout, and writer's block hadn't caused me to abandon writing.

On a wet, windy day, if I think too hard about how slippery it will be on the foredeck and how tricky it will be to set the whisker pole, nervousness seizes me. Instead, I move automatically, climbing up before my mind registers what's happening, before it tells my heart to race and my hands to shake. Muscle memory kicks in, and by trusting my body I can stop fear before it begins. But then, there's no shame in admitting to panic and despair, or in refusing when circumstances are too dangerous or difficult. There are some racecourses I haven't signed up for because they aren't meant for the kind of racing I want to do, and I can bypass them without regret.

Controlled Capsize

WEEK ONE LESSONS:
- Rigging and derigging
- Parts of the boat
- Body position and boat balance
- Steering basics
- Towing

Like ducklings following their mother, our Quest dinghies are being towed by our instructor's boat by mooring lines. My fellow students, who I'll call Max and Deniz, take turns on the tiller as Connor turns us in a circle. If we push the tiller in the wrong direction, the towing lines strain, the boat is off balance, and our hull knocks into the boat tied behind us. We circle around in the sheltered mooring area just beyond Toronto's National Yacht Club and avoid crashing into the sterns of the keelboats on either side of us. Three full-grown adults working in a stubby, fourteen-foot boat is awkward, yet the novelty of being so close to the water and the simple mechanics of pushing and pulling the tiller make up for that discomfort.

"Too bad we don't have sails up," Deniz says, and we agree. All six of the students in the course have some sailing experience—Deniz owns a boat here at NYC, Max used to race with his uncle and stopped only when he got a concussion, and the three younger women in the other boat have sailed with their families. I'm eager to rig the boat and to get out onto the lake—it's a warm, sparkling June morning, with a brisk but not gusty breeze. Maybe we'll impress our instructor, who's in his late twenties and tells us he's pleased to be teaching a group of adults rather than unruly kids and teenagers. He leads us through more exercises to get us familiar with the feel of the boat's buoyancy, our position and weight, before towing us back to the dinghy ramp.

The class costs $550 for non-members and $500 for NYC members, which is comparable to the fees at most sailing clubs around the lake. I chose this club for its proximity to my new apartment near Dundas West subway station, but I was still fifteen minutes late biking down to National, which is located at the bottom of Bathurst Street. When I arrived, I saw bags and jackets on the long tables inside a tent on the lawn, but no students. They were already by the dinghy shed with life jackets on. Had I missed the instruction portion? I have a feeling of lacking something necessary for the day, but I've brought nearly everything that National's program manager listed: lunch, spare clothing, hat, sunscreen, my boat shoes, and a notebook and pen. I don't have a PFD but there are plenty at the club to borrow.

We learn to rig the brand-new RS Quests, made of white moulded polyethylene, which make them very light. We'll later find their plastic hulls an advantage when we bump into each other beyond the breakwater. The Quests have narrow seats and edges that turn over in a lip that we can perch on. Unlike a keelboat, they have a centreboard that is lowered by pushing it down through a slot in the hull. Because there's relatively little weight in a centreboard, it's necessary to use one's bodyweight to counteract the force of the wind on the sails and the boat's heel. Dinghies are also more mobile; instead of being tied to a moor or slip, they are pushed onto a long dolly and stored on land, or what is known as "dry sail" storage areas in a yard or garage. They're a popular choice for sailing schools, and also for solo and double-handed racing, and among one-design fleets at the main community co-op dinghy clubs on the island and in the Outer Harbour. For example, the Toronto Island Sailing Club has a fleet of Albacores that are co-operatively owned by its members, who can sign the boats out for social sailing and race nights.

Dinghies are a much more affordable and accessible way to start sailing than buying a keelboat. Yet because these boats are very responsive and more "tippy," or prone to capsizing, sailing a dinghy well arguably requires a higher level of skill, balance, and courage. With just two or three students to a boat, I'm going to get lots of practice on the tiller. I wonder why I didn't sign up for a course years earlier. My learning experience in sailing has been completely backwards—most people take learn-to-sail classes when they're young and learn the theory and techniques that they can then apply to racing, crewing, and cruising. Because I began racing first, and am also on the helm so rarely, I'm still confused about many aspects of sailing theory, even after a decade of crewing. But it's never too late to sign up for a class, at any age.

Connor teaches us the parts of the boat and demonstrates how to find the jib halyard and attach it to the sail, how to feed the slugs along the edge of the main into the groove of the mast and the boom, how to make a loop with the main halyard to pass through the head of the sail and through the bobble, how to attach the outhaul. Even though we watch Connor carefully, it's still hard to keep track of all the lines and which way they should pass through the sails. It's also a little worrisome to me how thin the halyards are compared to those on a larger keelboat—will they really be able to handle all the force on them?

We break for classroom instruction and lunch before heading out. Connor draws a diagram on a tiny whiteboard, triangulating speed, balance, and steering. Speed is controlled through the main and jib sails, balance through the body positions of the helmsperson and crew, and steering through the tiller and rudder. Sailing a dinghy requires all three working together. After lunch, Connor checks that everything is properly rigged before we pull the trailers down the ramp, the crisp new sails flapping and making the booms wave back and forth in the wind. One by one, we climb carefully into the hull, fitting in the rudder and pushing down the centreboard as he tows us through the mooring area and past the breakwater. After detaching the towing lines, we are finally sailing.

My mood rights itself. In May 2022, I moved back to Toronto after eight months as writer-in-residence at the University of New Brunswick. Toronto seems angrier than I remembered, and the noise of honking horns and early-morning buses feeds into my newly rented ground floor apartment. There's a bar whose back patio faces the alleyway outside my window, and on random evenings it sounds like there's a party next door. Before I left Toronto at the end of last August, *Panache*'s crew toasted me with beers on the clubhouse patio as though

I were going away for good. This gave me a misplaced feeling that I ought to have stayed in New Brunswick, rented a
quaint house by the Bay of Fundy or in Saint John, a feeling
that is worsened by the changes in Toronto since the pandemic. Fortunately, the lake still offers the same ample views.

Connor leads us through two drills, the Figure Eight and
Follow the Leader. We circle around two buoys in a figure-eight pattern to practise steering and using our weight,
and then we follow Connor as his motorized dinghy drives
in a curving path. Deniz is on the tiller, and I'm also on the
windward side, with Max balancing out the boat and handling
sail trim. I'm reassured that both of them appear so competent, but at the same time, I feel annoyed at myself that I'm
not taking more initiative. Deniz tacks quickly, and before he
and I can cross to the windward side, our combined weight
tips the hull over and slides us both into the lake. The water
is the temperature of a lukewarm bath, but the plunge is like
waking up suddenly from a vivid dream. Max manages to
hold on to the lip of the hull and land on top of it, and hardly
gets wet at all. He quickly steps on the centreboard so that the
Quest springs back up. We haul each other over the transom
and Connor checks in on us.

"I think Phoebe's in shock," Deniz says as I sit blinking in
silence. In fact, I am furious. I don't show it or say it, but I blame
him for not giving us more warning before tacking. Once
Connor ascertains that we're okay, he instructs us to continue
with the drills. But I notice that we seem to be sitting lower and
lower in the water, with the lake licking up into the bow. What
if this brand-new dinghy sinks into the lake on our very first day
of class? None of us know what to do, and Connor motors over
to us, checking the transom drains with puzzlement.

"One of you climb aboard with me," he tells us, "and see if you can sail back to the dock." Max, Deniz, and I look at each other.

"Do you want to go with Connor?" Deniz asks me, full of concern, but I shake my head. "You weigh more, and you're sitting closer," I say. Hearing something in my voice, he climbs out of the Quest and into the inflatable dinghy that motors off to direct the girls in the other boat.

On the tiller, Max points the boat directly at the breakwater and we sail on a reach toward it. "I don't really know where the wind is," Max admits, but while the air feels very light, the sails aren't luffing and so we keep to our current bearing. "You're doing great," I reply, adjusting the main. The distance isn't far—on a keelboat it would take minutes to reach the entrance between the rocks, but our small boat is only going a few knots. After we make it through the breakwater and tie up the dinghy, Max steps onto the dock, legs suddenly folding under him. "I need a moment," he says, his limbs shaking, as though the stress has caught up to him.

When I come back after changing, I help haul the Quest up the ramp. It's much heavier than it should be, and water starts streaming out once it's tilted on its dolly. "The plug was missing on it," Connor explains, even though he had inspected the boats the evening before. I realize the boat had been taking on water from the beginning and that is likely why we capsized.

There's so much water in the hull that Connor estimates it'll take several hours to drain out. I'm now glad I didn't blame Deniz when we capsized. My irritation shifts to our instructor for not being more vigilant. "It's very hard to sail when the hull is full of water," Connor tells us, raising his brows at me and Max. I can't tell if he's impressed or not, but

I start to think I'm going to do all right in the course.

WEEK TWO LESSONS:
- Points of sail and sail trim
- Port tack and starboard tack
- Heading up and bearing off
- Windward and leeward
- How to find wind direction
- Local hazards
- Tacking and gybing

This week, we're two to a boat. I'm paired with Audra, a young woman in her twenties with curly hair, glasses, and a keen air about her. We barely know each other but we make a good team. Audra's more confident helming while I'm more knowledgeable with trimming sails. This week, Connor gives us drills on how to tack and gybe, and we take turns handling the tiller and mainsheet together. With just two of us in the boat, I can feel its lightness and buoyancy, the way it's supposed to feel when the hull isn't full of water. I've already told the story of my first class to anyone who would listen. My friends, family, and co-workers are horrified, but every other sailor tells me they've either gone through the same trial or experienced worse ones.

Just below Ontario Place, the lake's current swirls about in a kind of bowl. National members have nicknamed this area the "washing machine," which I wish I'd known earlier because shifty breezes baffle students still learning how to steer a boat. Audra has a thirst for speed but isn't quite able to find the wind direction yet, nor does she know how to trim sails for speed. I, on the other hand, know what a boat is supposed to feel like when it's heeling and close-hauled, but I'm reluctant to steer closer to the wind because I know how essential boat balance and body position are, and I don't want to capsize in a gust. Audra can also nimbly cross to the other side when tacking, managing to hold the awkwardly long tiller extension behind her while passing the mainsheet to the other hand, but she tends to stall midway through the tacks because she hasn't accelerated enough. I have the opposite problem. While I pull in the main to gather the necessary speed, much to Audra's delight, I can't seem to tack without dropping the mainsheet. I struggle with crossing the boat when the tiller is jammed against my back or hip. I either fall over or overtack—or both. Audra's so busy watching me and giving advice that she forgets to sheet in the jib, backwinding the boat until I gently remind her to face forward.

It's also new to me to be giving commands or instructions while helming. The role of teacher is much more comfortable for me—I'm currently teaching my first creative writing course as a sessional instructor. I'm finding that I enjoy giving lectures on creative protagonists, on form poetry, and on narrative. I don't write the lectures out beforehand. I can easily fill an hour talking about craft, and the longer I speak, the more I'm able to make connections and the more meanings become clearer to me. I begin to look forward to a kind of deepening turn, when speech, instead of feeling like an imperfect approximation, is a map with several routes. After my lectures, I felt strange, surprised, drained, and energized at the same time.

During my years of tutoring and teaching ESL, I noted that students appreciated simple directives they could easily absorb and put into practice, that they required a lot of repetition of new information, and that repetition should take as many forms as possible. My teacher's training emphasized that if the student did not understand, it was the instructor who had failed. After exhausting the strategies in the instructor's manual and still encountering blank looks from my students, I found better explanations and examples when thinking on the fly. An instructors' attitude can also affect the students' morale and confidence. A sarcastic, condescending tone only makes students feel stupid and unmotivated. I think of simple ways to get Audra to remember to trim the jib, such as keeping in mind that the main and jib should be at roughly the same angle. Getting annoyed when she backwinds the jib yet again won't make her learn any faster.

Connor's teaching is light on theory and classroom instruction, and we only spend a short period in the tent before he gets on a dinghy to demonstrate a manoeuvre. We practise for a few hours with drills before a lunch break, then we debrief, and then we hit the lake again for the afternoon, followed by derigging and another debrief based on what he's observed on the water. He only loosely follows the order of the eight lessons laid out in our course materials, adjusting them to our abilities. We're taught what roles the helm and the crew have in tacking and gybing, who communicates what, how to trim the main, where to position our bodies to balance the boat, and how to trim again after a tack or gybe.

On the water, our boats line up in a row, pointing into the wind and facing Connor's dinghy. He instructs us to accelerate on the same tack, and when he blows the whistle, we all tack. After about a minute, he blows the whistle again, repeating the drill as we zigzag upwind.

"Ready to tack?" Audra says to me at each toot of the whistle. "Ready," I say, grabbing the jib sheets, ready to release.

"Helm's a-lee," she calls out energetically, pushing the tiller behind her as the boom swings across and I cleat in the taut jib sheet. When it's my turn helming, the short intervals between tacks don't give me time to overthink or to get nervous, and the repetition of the drill helps to build muscle memory. I still sometimes drop the main, but I get better at not overtacking. Knowing that Connor's dinghy is directly upwind also removes the work of having to figure out wind direction. By looking to an imaginary point ninety degrees away, perhaps at a boat or buoy in the distance, I can stop and straighten the tiller once the boat is pointed where I want. It's a simple action, looking to where I want to be.

We're taught the difference between a controlled and uncontrolled gybe. What we want to avoid while going downwind is the boom flying across in a wind shift. The boom might not be heavy enough to knock the crew overboard, but we don't want to test that. Connor circles around and we line up, going downwind, and once again we turn the stern through the wind each time he blows the whistle. As one of us communicates the intention to gybe and starts to bear off, the other flips the boom over as the helm sheets in the main slightly, straightens out the tiller, and lets out the sail after the gybe is completed. We practise with the Figure Eight drill, gybing at the two points at the top and the bottom of the figure, occasionally bumping into other boats.

When Connor calls out for us to return to the dock, I'm surprised it's nearly four o'clock already. Heading back to the breakwater, we practise our new skills as he collects the buoys. This time is nearly as valuable, if not more, than the supervised drills. I look in the direction I want the boat to be pointed at, but once I tack, the boat ends up in the opposite direction and I'm disoriented. I'm still confused about when I should tack, head up, or bear off toward my destination. I stare at the entrance through the rocks, determined to get there.

WEEK THREE LESSONS:
- Knots: figure eight, reef, bowline, and other important knots
- Capsizing and recovering
- Hypothermia and heat stroke
- Stopping and accelerating

It's such a gusty day that Connor teaches us some basic knots, hoping the wind will ease up by mid-morning. The sheet bend is new to me, and very useful for tying together two lines of different weights. The round turn with two half hitches is good for tying on a fender or securing a line to a post, and the cleat hitch is another simple knot for attaching a line on a boat for docking and towing. We learn the symptoms and treatment for hypothermia and heat stroke, knowledge that is particularly applicable to living in Canada, with its extreme weather.

Knowing that we've paid to have on-the-water time for four weeks, Connor might have little choice but to take us out. This week, a club photographer will take our pictures as we practise heading up and bearing off. Audra's not in class today so I join the two other girls, who I'll call Madeline and Emma, in rigging the Quests. Madeline and Emma have just graduated, and their eyes widen when I tell them I'm a creative writing instructor. One of us takes the helm, another manages the reefed main, and the third is seated near the jib sheets. Our helming abilities are about equal, but trimming sails is my happy place. Unlike Audra, Madeleine and Emma are more nervous about the boat heeling in the gusty wind. When it's my turn to helm, I tell them to ease the sails to depower the boat and to reduce heel, even though I'm tempted to see what the Quest can do. With a long tiller extension and hiking straps, I can see they're designed to be speedy. I hope one day to be able to hike out on the high side, nudging the tiller as I've seen other Star and Laser sailors do during a race.

Because it's too windy further out on the lake, we practise rounding marks just beyond the breakwater. As I pull the tiller through a tack, once again we don't move our weight quickly enough and the boat flips us into the lake. This time, I'm much calmer—I'm prepared for what's happening because Connor has taken us through the capsize procedure. But I realize that Madeline and Emma may be in as much shock as I was a few weeks ago. I call out to them, and we each remember Connor's instruction: keep a hand on the boat at all times. The photographer starts capturing us as we grab the centreboard, right the boat, and awkwardly haul each other by the straps of our wet sleeves and life jackets over the transom. As the last one in, I take hold of the tiller, and Emma asks me to turn into irons. I'm surprised that I can do so without thinking hard about it, and we pause to catch our breaths. The warm sun dries us quickly, but Madeleine gets colder the longer we're out, and it's a relief when Connor instructs us to return to the dock and ends class early so we can warm ourselves with coffee and showers. "No one's going to want to sail with me again," I say to the girls, but they reassure me otherwise.

"I can't believe you went out," Amanda says to me later when I tell her about the class. Even at her dinghy club, St. James Town, most members had decided not to sail in such gusty conditions. She too has capsized numerous times, and I realize that it can happen to even experienced dinghy sailors. Later, when the photographer sends us the photos, I see three figures bundled in bulky PFDs. Their expressions are furrowed in concentration, their heads tilted to look at the sails. I recognize myself, hands adjusting the tiller, tugging on the main or holding out the boom. We look like we know what we're doing, or, at least, like we're on our way.

WEEK FOUR LESSONS:
- Sailing to a point
- Sail trim review
- Using your ticklers
- Sailing upwind and downwind
- Rounding windward and leeward mark
- Basic rules of right of way

Even though helming a dinghy tenses my body and floods my brain, I look forward to the next class. During the week, I replay the manoeuvres of tacking and gybing, itching for more practice. The weeks have gone by quickly and I review my notes in each debrief, where Connor has explained basic procedures that I haven't grasped in over a decade of racing. For instance, that getting a lift means a boat can head closer to the wind, and if there is wind in both directions, tacking is a good option.

He explains something called the centre of effort, which is the effort applied to the boat in the form of the wind's force on the sail that moves the boat forward, counteracted by the centre of lateral resistance below the boat, with the drag created by the centreboard and rudder. The combination of the two is what the boat uses to move forward. I only partially understand, but this is only a CANSail 1 class, the first stage of Sail Canada's six-level program. These topics aren't included on our skills checklist and might go over our heads, but they also keep our interest by giving us a taste of what's to come. I realize I've done the same thing with my students, speaking about approaches to craft or writing that might be too complex or contradictory for where they're at in their practices. My hope is that some among them already do have the capacity, or that it'll make sense to them later on, or that it'll motivate them to keep writing.

For our last class, we practise sailing an upwind and downwind course. Audra is back this week, and we try to keep in mind everything we've learned—keeping our tacks close to the course, which is more efficient than one long tack, keeping the main close-hauled, keeping the boat heeling to leeward, and ensuring that the helmsperson is always on the windward side, which gives them a better view of the course. When sailing downwind, we need to watch for accidental gybes and luffing sails. We're also going to practise mark roundings, sailing to the layline and bearing off when we reach the windward mark, and heading up and sheeting in when rounding the windward mark. All of these procedures are things I've been instructed to do for years by my skippers, and now that I'm on the helm myself, I find it extremely useful to go through these manoeuvres step by step. My familiarity with racecourses is a huge advantage. As soon as marks are dropped, I feel more confident helming than I am without any specific destination. A course relieves my mind from decision fatigue and tells me where the wind is coming from.

My recent career opportunities, such as doing the residency at UNB, joining poetry editorial boards, and teaching, make me feel grateful and, at the same time, a loss of control. These opportunities have affected where I live and travel, how I schedule my time, who I meet. I feel like I can accept the courses others envision for me as long I keep my long-term goal of sustaining my life as a writer in sight, which is a much more difficult course to plot.

Audra and I each practise going around the upwind/downwind course that Connor sets up for us. Like on a racecourse, we had been instructed to sail parallel to the start line before heading up, to plan our tacks toward the windward mark, to go through a controlled gybe after rounding the mark, and then to stop the boat once we return to the start line. I let Audra know that she was still not accelerating enough before tacking and that she also tacked more often than necessary to reach the mark, but otherwise, she ably rounded the course with her usual confidence. When it was my turn, I plotted out the number of tacks I would need to round the mark to port and managed to keep my balance and not to overtack as we headed upwind. Halfway on the downwind leg, I felt the boat tip slightly to windward and I instructed Audra to pull the boom across as I gybed the Quest and continued across to the finish line, where I sheeted in the sails and turned us into irons. Rounding the course had only taken a few minutes.

"That was perfect!" Audra exclaimed. I grinned back at her. Despite having bigger accomplishments, rounding a course on a dinghy without any major errors or mishaps puffed me up with pride and satisfaction. The points of sail made sense to me in a simple, embodied way, and I wondered how I had ever not known them. This was like learning to read or to bike—once I'd developed those abilities, I couldn't recreate the lack of them. Later, as I took the helm after a Wednesday-night race on *Panache*, I eased the sails onto a reach. "I've never seen Phoebe steer so well," Mark said. "It's almost like she's taken a course." Mark was too far away for me to swat, and I couldn't reach him without letting go of the tiller. Perhaps I would learn how to do that in CANSail 2.

There were still a few remaining tasks to complete before we ended the afternoon with Connor delivering our class debriefs, one-on-one feedback, and CANSail skills check-list. Audra had been the only student who hadn't practised the capsize procedure, so I climbed aboard Connor's dinghy so she could do it unassisted. With aplomb, Audra stood up and stepped onto the lip of the boat until it tipped and turtled. She swam without panic toward the centreboard, but she wasn't heavy or strong enough to right it immediately. Connor motored closer to assist, but in doing so, overturned the boat again. This didn't faze Audra—she once again put her feet on the centreboard and, as the hull tipped, stamped on it with her full weight until it popped back up and she was able to climb triumphantly on board.

Learning how to right a capsized boat might not have practical applications when living in an environment like Toronto's—I might have believed that once. Now I can think of the many times in my life when I needed to know how to recover a vessel and get back on course. Still not quite sure what I mean? It'll make sense later.

Time Elapsed,
Corrected Time

1. Club race results require a certain literacy, as does everything related to racing sailboats. After a race, results are posted in tidy columns with fleets, classes, boat names, names of the skipper, sail numbers, and PHRF ratings, along with dates, start, and finish times. It's peppered with acronyms such as DNF, which stands for Did Not Finish, which may imply that the wind shut off halfway up the course. DNC, or Did Not Compete or did not come to the starting area, could mean that the skipper was away at the cottage. A DNS, or Did Not Start, means a boat made it to the racecourse but did not cross the start line, perhaps due to equipment malfunction, whereas RAF, or RET, Retired after Finish, can be scored if a skipper realized they had broken a rule without taking their penalty. There's a story behind every use of these acronyms, and I go in search of them.

2. In a video of the first race of the 2018 season, I'm holding the edge of the headsail as the bow of the boat is turning through the wind. As Mark pushes the tiller leeward, I lift the sail over my head and let it go to fill out on the windward side as we round the red marker buoy. Phil effortlessly sheets in the jib while Mark straightens the tiller and Pat adjusts the main. We do our tasks synchronously and competently, with little instruction. Mark has begun bragging that we are the best crew at the club, which I always deny, perhaps out of a superstitious fear. Still vivid in my memory is the phase in our racing career when we wrapped the jib the wrong way around the winch, fumbled with the whisker pole, were overwhelmed with making a couple of quick tacks toward the upwind mark. Our videos are less entertaining, Mark says, now that we all know what we're doing.

3. I noted the seconds and minutes of our time elapsed and time corrected, replaying what I remember of the race in my mind, trying to assess where we might've lost five, ten, twenty seconds. Likely Mark and the others do the same, but we try not to dwell on the results. Each race is so distinct in terms of wind direction and weather that every week is like turning a page. The lake is unmarked by our performances, wiped blank afterwards.

4. I experience time in segments, some seamlessly running together, others that abruptly start and end. I measure my own life not in years or months but in these phases; I feel that time is experienced collectively in epochs and eras. The past, present, and future feel like subtle shades in bars

of sand, a spectrum of greys and crushed minerals, and so difficult to demarcate. "The end of an era," some might say as neon lights shutter at the closing of a storied venue, when roommates vacate a house ashy with parties, or a community disbands like droplets from an evaporating cloud. I'm suspicious of nostalgia, because looking back makes me ache for the present. Each sailing season feels bright and continuous, but I'm aware that up ahead is a blurry gradation between something ending and something else beginning. At some point, circumstances will toss this settled period into new configurations, but it feels too distant for me to think of cataloguing the quality of stippled light, the precise textures and darting feelings. The present then feels sharper, more delicately painful.

5. Looking over a decade of race results, I see how quickly we improved from series to series, season to season. Even in the first few years, *Panache* usually placed in the top half of the fleet in overall results, quite often a respectable third. We were winning flags from our very first season and have never missed the Champion of Champions race, an end-of-the-season race that only those who have placed in the top three of each fleet are eligible to participate in. We learned fast and recovered from our errors quickly, since we were young and energetic. The years were kind and expansive to us.

6. In its Handicappers Manual Bylaws, Performance Handicap Racing Fleet of Lake Ontario (PHRF-LO) describes its handicap system as "an equitable system of handicaps based upon speed potential and observed

performance of monohull sailboats." This gives two parameters for calculating handicaps. Race participants are divided into PHRF fleets, because it would be neither fair nor feasible for eighty boats of varying models to start a race at the same time. The slowest boats, the Sharks and Stars, start first, followed by the smaller keelboats, then the larger keelboats. The idea is that faster boats will require less time to round the course, so the race committee can record finishing times and calculate results within a reasonable window of time. It's like running a race against a younger sibling and letting them have a five-minute head start because they're smaller and have shorter legs.

7. I have always had the inexplicable sense that my time sailing on *Panache* is finite, and the thought evokes the ache I have known when I couldn't return to some place of contingent familiarity.

8. While knowing a boat's PHRF rating is helpful for getting an idea of its performance on the water, the rating isn't the whole story. Fleets may have size ranges, but because of the rig, condition of sails, and amount of crew experience, it can transpire that a smaller boat, like a J22, is rated high enough to compete against the PHRF 1 fleet of bigger thirty-foot keelboats. Racers learn to size up the competition—they literally look at the cut of their jibs. I squint at how crisp and new the sails appear to be and note whether the boat is fully crewed or shorthanded. These are indicators of how a boat will perform relative to the rest of the fleet. In a mixed fleet, there can be so

many varying factors that, in a sense, each boat is racing against its past performances, or against some theoretical performance of the boat's optimal racing potential.

9. Crouching on the bow as the boat tacked through the wind and leaning over to catch the edge of the jib to skirt it against the lifelines. Moving to the high side and extending my legs when I felt the boat heel in a gust. Ensuring all the lines were clear as our crew eased out the sails on a broad reach or dead downwind before reaching over to push out the boom. Tucking the whisker pole under my arm while throwing a flapping genoa over my head. These actions became automatic after several seasons of racing. On average, going around the course three or four times took *Panache* about forty minutes to an hour, depending on the amount of wind, but I was rarely aware of the race time elapsing when I was on the boat. Sometimes I was surprised by how quickly we beat upwind, other times the minutes crawled as we rounded the mark and tried to ascertain which side to pole out the indecisive jib. As long as we were moving and the boat making progress, time felt stretchy and inestimable.

10. I returned from a trip to Europe in late June of 2018 eager to sail again, about to enter a full-time position at OCAD U, and wrapping up the promotion for my first book. Race nights grounded my hectic and variable schedule, and I was grateful for the familiarity of my role on *Panache*. But by next season, I was growing restless. I knew I was contributing on the foredeck, but I wanted a more active role. I itched to be trimming sails, but we already had an

extremely competent crew on the main and the jib. I knew it benefited *Panache* when I undertook the same tasks I always did on the bow—it showed in the race results, the accumulation of flags, the improvement in *Panache*'s PHRF rating. I found plenty to learn through observation, but in hindsight I can see that I was nearing the end of a phase without being aware of it. It rose beneath me, like the surface of the lake pitching under everything that it carried.

11. Early May 2020. Spring in Toronto was as replete as always, trees thick with buds, dregs of crusty snow washing away, the air softening. I saw my neighbours on my walks down to the Humber River trail as they dug up gardens, skipped behind their retrievers and terriers, carried small children on their shoulders. It was like any other spring, except it wasn't. In windows and on porches hung homemade sheets and signs, painted with hearts and handprints, thanking health care workers. At seven in the evening, the streets rattled and banged with the noise of pots and pans and drums. I breathed in the smell of spring rain through a cloth mask. The loop of the seasons was the same, but somehow we had been pushed off course.

12. Every boat that wishes to race at QCYC, and at regattas around the Great Lakes, must apply for a PHRF certificate. They do so by submitting a long list of boat measurements, with assistance from the club's measurement team and PHRF-LO Handicapper. The club measurers determine the rating for each boat by identifying whether it is a class boat or a custom boat. A class boat can have several manufacturers producing the same model of boat,

whereas a custom boat is a unique design usually produced in limited quantities. Each of these can also appear
as a standard boat—that is, one in good condition with
a set of standard-sized sails, a mast, and an engine, or
it might have been modified by the owner in substantial ways, with a heavier or lighter keel, mast and boom
length changes, or differently sized sails. Once the measurers have given the boat a temporary rating with adjustments, they forward the applications to PHRF-LO to be
published online and verified. It's possible to look up the
rating of every boat registered, to see how your own boat
might measure against them in a race, or to look into the
racing potential of a boat you wish to purchase. To imagine how it might perform compared to others once you've
factored in your own expertise.

13. Campuses closed across the country, and as I crammed
files into my knapsack and flicked off my desk lamp in the
empty office, I believed we'd be back in a few months. At
home, on my laptop screen, my co-workers appeared in
their small boxes. Some of them I wouldn't meet in person
for another two and a half years. Between long days of
online meetings, I paced around the backyard, my shoes
sinking into the softening ground. My fingers grazed new
buds and neighbourhood cats. Time had a weight to it,
pressing down on my chest. Minutes and hours dripped
like melting ice into the sewers and flowed away from me.

14. Any other year, weekends in May meant sanding and
painting in boatyards. Senior members at Queen City
Yacht Club would be getting up early, putting on their

overalls and wool sweaters to heave and push the boats in their cradles down the rail and into the lagoon. With the province in an extended state of emergency from mid-March until mid-May, social gatherings were restricted and all non-essential businesses and outdoor recreational amenities closed. Launch was postponed indefinitely. QCYC's board members and staff communicated that both the clubhouse and the yard would remain closed except for essential maintenance and flood mitigation work. Amid a global pandemic, concerns over the cancellation of a sailing season felt unimportant, even frivolous. Every other year, I'd counted down the days to launch. Without anything to anticipate, the weeks and months ran together. Even when there were no changes to the situation, Ron Mazza, the commodore that year, regularly provided updates—board meeting minutes, summaries of ongoing work at the club, member surveys, and club COVID-19 protocols provided a sense of progress and were a means of measuring time when the waiting made its own interminable season.

15. A PHRF rating represents a boat's speed potential in seconds over nautical miles, a number that is relative to an arbitrary, theoretical boat with a rating of zero seconds per mile. The higher the PHRF rating, the slower the boat. I have seen people use temperature measurements to help explain the concept of using an arbitrary benchmark to set your standard zero rating. For instance, the Celsius scale sets zero degrees to represent water's freezing point and one hundred degrees its boiling point—it's a relative scale and not an absolute one. A boat's PHRF

rating, therefore, is not static. It's a performance-based indicator. The club's race results must also be sent to PHRF-LO at the end of each season, and a boat's rating may be updated. A rating is always in multiples of three, acknowledging that the rating process isn't accurate enough to justify increments of one second/mile. It doesn't take into account factors like the condition of the boat and its sails, the knowledge and experience of its crew, and local wind and weather conditions. Like many attempts at equity, it's flawed, since no two boats, even of the same model, are exactly the same.

16. The feeling of loss felt like layers and layers of blankets and I struggled beneath them. It's surprising to me now that I got out of bed at all to make coffee and log onto Teams, check emails, put away groceries. I love solitude, but this kind of loneliness steeped underneath doors and into my notebooks and drawers. I knew that I was luckier than most. I hadn't lost my job, I was in good physical health, my parents were retired and had no need to go out except for essentials, and I was without dependants. I easily imagined much greater losses.

17. At the end of April, Doug Ford, premier of Ontario, announced that boats could prepare to launch at marinas, and within a week, the City of Toronto gave QCYC permission to consider itself a marina. By mid-May, boat clubs were allowed to open if they were prepared to and the members were surveyed about their preferences. In early June, the board began proposing a process for launch to begin with strict COVID-19 protocols. Timelines are

imperfect. The gaps between emails, announcements, and updates were like contractions between a heartbeat. I don't recall the date when, one spring evening, someone emailed the club to say their partner was too ill to launch their boat. Or when one member, on the island on their assigned day, paused in the yard to stare blankly into space, disoriented with gladness.

18. At the end of July, Mark sent an email asking Pat, Phil, Tim, Quentin, Amanda, and me if we would be interested in racing on Wednesday nights. I'd been waiting for this email for many months, and all of us were enthusiastically a "yes." We wore face masks when we rode the ferry or tender and on the club grounds, and only removed them when we were on the boat and leaving the dock. Seeing my fellow crew members again, sitting on the swaying bow of *Panache*, I felt as though a span of time had been given back to me.

19. What if people could be assigned PHRF certificates? What if there was some theoretical benchmark that we could compare ourselves to?

20. When racing in a mixed fleet using the PHRF system, a boat's ranking is based on its corrected time, not the time elapsed. The time elapsed during the race is the time between the race committee's sounding for a start of the race and when a boat crosses the finish line, and once that time has been adjusted to factor in their handicap, its corrected time is recorded. For instance, on a Wednesday-night race in August 2020, *Panache* started the race with

the PHRF 3 fleet at 18:26:00 and crossed the finish line about an hour later, at 19:35:25, for a total elapsed time of 1:09:25. The race committee plugged these times into the Sailwave software to calculate a corrected time of 1:05:36. The software multiplies a boat's elapsed time by a time-correction factor using a formula provided by PHRF-LO to generate race results. Not being a mathematician or a computer scientist, I cannot parse the lines of code that make up the formula, but I am content for this conversion method and time-correction factor to remain indecipherable to me.

21. It wasn't possible to hold a normal race series when the race committee couldn't socially distance on the cramped *Freddy M*. Instead, after dropping the marks for the start line north of the lawn by the clubhouse, the race committee returned to the club. They arranged themselves in front of the clubhouse, masks on and binoculars in hand, calling out start times on the radio. We raced a triangle course every week, starting from north of the clubhouse, going to an orange mark dropped near Polson Quay, across the harbour to the EKO-15 Channel buoy south of the York Street slip, and back toward the start line. We showed up for the six races with the same crew and the same race-course, but with variations in wind and weather conditions that would give us a rare reaching or downwind start if the wind was coming from the west or southwest. The repetition helped me to better understand the points of sail and anticipate each manoeuvre around the course. The body knows where it's been before, what it has done before, and recognizes when you ask the same thing of it.

22. QCYC uses the Time on Time method, and not the Time on Distance method, of calculating a boat's corrected time after a race. But on the water, it can be easier to approximate how *Panache* will rank using the Time on Distance method. For instance, *Panache's* rating in 2020 was 198. If we were racing against *Fine Wine*, a Northern 25 with a rating of 240, we would "owe" that boat time. The difference between the two ratings is 42 seconds, which means that *Panache* would owe 42 seconds for each nautical mile of the racecourse. So in a five-mile racecourse, *Panache* needs to finish 210 seconds—or three and a half minutes—ahead of *Fine Wine* to come out ahead. I have to admit I have found it frustrating to owe slower boats so much time, but it has worked out to our advantage when racing against bigger keelboats. In a mixed fleet, you can never be sure of the outcome of the race, so it's best not to celebrate too early, nor to become too convinced of your defeat.

23. From that point on, I set an intention to race every chance I could get. It made the rest of the week, with its devastating news and the world in suspension, more bearable. Not merely bearable—racing inserted lightness and fun back into my life when it was in such limited supply. I'd missed the time spent on water, in the open air, concentrating on a few simple but engrossing tasks. I multiplied the time I hadn't spent sailing by an unknown factor, but I couldn't convert these inputs into a result. The formula doesn't work that way. A participant can only be scored for races they have, at the very least, started, not those they intended to show up for. But

I wasn't penalized for the time I had missed. My speed potential remained the same.

24. When I multiplied the elapsed time of the pandemic years and the ensuing social isolation by a time-correction factor, what resulted was not a precise result. Instead, I obtained a span of time with blurry edges. Late winter days packing my bag for work were deducted. Cool spring Saturdays at the club were deducted, as were evenings around a picnic table, flicking off the sticky buds. We were living—are living—on corrected time, on time we owed to others, and will always be owed.

Buried Timber

I'M LOOKING FOR CLINDINNING Row. It's a row of boat builders, sailing clubs, and rowing clubs on the vanished wharves of Toronto's Victorian harbourfront. One summer evening in 1889, a group of sailors met in a boathouse locker to discuss the formation of a new sailing club that would become the Queen City Yacht Club. "History doesn't record the atmosphere upstairs over the dinghy lockers in the boathouse at 99 and 100 Clindinning Row on July 17, 1889," wrote the late club historian and journalist Wayne Lilley. Thanks to his rigorously researched centennial history of the club, I can come up with an approximate location of Clindinning Row—south of Union Station, at the foot of York Street. It's an area I know well, criss-crossed by streetcar tracks, sandwiched by Queen's Quay Terminal and Harbour Square Park West. Yet despite the factualness of Lilley's work, I'm not satisfied. I'm in search of what is omitted from the records.

Clindinning doesn't appear on any current map of Toronto, though it sounds like it should. It's a surname of Scottish and Irish origins with many variations, such as Glendinning, Glendon, and Clendenan, which are attached to current roads and areas traversed by early immigrants. Though maps are meant for wayfinding, I can also lose myself in them, in the scale they commit to, the rigorous naming. I collect museum floor plans, tourist maps with exaggerated landmarks, and gentle, muted illustrated maps of gardens. I want to live in the revelation that takes place when a map's approximation and the place that is being mapped meet and dissolve into each other. It's impossible to orient oneself by maps only, but nonetheless, I keep making the attempt.

Clicking through an online repository of Toronto maps, I'm disoriented by history. There's no Gardiner or Don Valley Parkway. Ashbridge's Bay is marshland, and from the mouth of the Don to the Humber, numerous wharves crowd the harbourfront. The arteries of the Grand Trunk Railway run from east to west and branch outward along routes that will become subway and streetcar tracks. I pore over city engineer and fire insurance maps, but they don't show me streetscapes, warehouses, or horse carriages. The Toronto of the 1880s and 1890s exists only in street names, remnants of architecture, brickwork quarries now filled in by ponds, and the pale inks of the archive.

In each of these maps, I start, like many Toronto visitors, at Union Station. I zoom in, trying to locate Clendinning Row, or any street south of the station. But I hadn't realized that today's Union Station is the third iteration of the building, evidence of the city's early tendency to outgrow and remake its landmarks. The first was built in 1853 just west of the current station's train shed at Station and Front Streets. But the three single-storey buildings with gently sloping roofs were no longer big enough to meet Toronto's population surge in the 1870s and were replaced in 1873 by a grand Second Empire–style building designed by architect Thomas Seaton Scott. It's a block-wide stone building with three towers, a clock face, Palladian windows, and decorative embellishments. This Union Station faced south on the corner of Esplanade West and Simcoe, highlighting the importance of water transportation at that time. To the south, on these Victorian maps, I find the Royal Canadian Yacht Club, Toronto Canoe Club, and the Argonaut Rowing Club perched at the former shoreline.

These maps also show wharves that no longer exist stretching out in the lake. I try to imagine Toronto's lakeshore messy with warehouses, sheds, and boat traffic. Wharves were used for sailboats and steamboats, cargo, passenger traffic, rescue operations, and printing operations, acting as the vestibule of the city. In pen-and-ink drawings, watercolours, lithographs, steel engravings, and images from developed glass plate negatives, the waterfront of Victorian Toronto looks like a rough, active place. Like a shifting set of tiles, the city's streets and landmarks flip over in a centuries-long game, revealing new configurations. Even as the grid of property lots, warehouses, factories, government buildings, courthouses, roads, and wharves were filling up, they were also being revised and redrawn.

Present-day Toronto residents grieve the city's lost and buried sites, trying to locate them again. The buried creeks. The lakeshore trail of the 1790s, which followed the topography from the sandbar that led to the islands to the Grenadier Pond to the Humber, used by Indigenous peoples and early settlers. The waterfront wharves demolished when the shoreline extended. The Toronto Historical Association lists 250 "lost sites," places that have been buried, demolished, or destroyed by fire—in the burning of York in 1813, in the Great Fire of Toronto in 1849, and the Second Great Fire of Toronto in 1904 that razed a hundred buildings in the industrial centre. Today, iconic buildings continue to be threatened by condo development or city planning. Toronto residents, dazed by the speed of construction, fight to preserve the city's beloved landmarks, but the maps show that restlessness has been a feature of this city since its beginnings. Everywhere you go in Toronto, something is buried. I realize I'm looking for more than an address or the location of Queen City's former clubhouses. I'm hoping that the club's history and origins might give me a better understanding of how I fit in. How to orient myself.

I'm familiar with the Toronto Purchase of 1787, but I'm still unsettled by one 1805 map of Toronto. The city is but an outline, a black rectangle stretching from Lake Ontario to King Street, covering the 250,808 acres of the Toronto Purchase. The delicately drawn Carrying Place route is the only road on the map, implying a void to be filled. The 1813 "Williams Sketch of the ground in advance of and including York Upper Canada" map shows a small grid of streets in the centre of York, as Toronto was then called, and estates and farms to the city's west, surrounded by woodland and bush. The growth of the city accelerates and becomes denser through the decades. In the "1851 J. O. Browne Map of the Township of York," the land has been divided into concessions and lots. Nathan Ng, who has collected the online archive of Toronto maps, writes that the 1850s land-boom era was a time of prosperity when speculators bought, sold, and subdivided lots for profit. The maps of this period, made by civil servants, engineers, and licensed surveyors, reveal the results of constant construction. The Parliament Buildings, Government House and City Hall, the older Garrison and new Garrison, University of Toronto, the Royal Observatory (also known as the Magnetic Observatory), Osgoode Hall, and the Provincial Lunatic Asylum, which is today's Centre for Addiction and Mental Health building on Queen Street, became Toronto's fixed landmarks.

At last, on an 1889 fire insurance map, I see *W. H. Clindinning* written below *Boat Builder* across a rectangular building. These fire insurance maps are the most detailed that I've found. The notations *Canoe Club* and *Boat Club* may refer to Toronto Canoe Club, Royal Canadian Yacht Club, or the Argonaut Rowing Club. Some letters are in ink, others in careful pencil. The QCYC website houses archival materials, including 1890 images of simple, two-storey boathouses with sturdy pitched roofs and what look like rows of leaded windows. Union Station's tower adorns the background. I enlist current Queen City club historian Richard Slee to help me locate the boat lockers of Clindinning Row. He informs me that not only have the streets and buildings changed, but the waterfront has as well—Toronto's waterfront used to be located at Front Street, about a kilometre from its present-day location.

"The City has created additional room by filling in the waterfront since the early days of the 1850s when you started to see the advent of the railways. By the 1890s it had made its way down to Lake Street with the old Union Station just to the north over the rail lines," he emails me, surmising that today, Clindinning Row would now be located between Simcoe and York Streets, just under the present Gardiner Expressway. Which means that every time I walked south to the bottom of York Street and waited impatiently at the pedestrian crossings before the Gardiner on-ramp, I was unknowingly stepping over the very roots of the club.

Yacht clubs proliferated along the eastern seaboard from the mid-1800s, signalling the settler and immigrant population's growing prosperity and desire for recreation. The oldest yacht club in North America is the Royal Nova Scotia Yacht Squadron, founded in 1837, and the Detroit Boat Club, formed two years after in 1839, followed by the New York Yacht Club in 1844, home of America's Cup. The Royal Canadian Yacht Club had its beginnings as the Toronto Boat Club in 1850, undergoing a few name changes before moving to Toronto Islands in 1881. By that time, the Bay of Quinte Yacht Club had been formed and running for five years in Belleville, Ontario, organizing the first Lake Yacht Racing Association (LYRA) race in August 1885. These early clubs, which began with a few dozen members, are still operating today. The previous Victorian generation had incorporated the town of York into the city of Toronto, transforming "Muddy York" into a hub of industry with markets, paved roads, and gas lamps. Residents built Georgian-style manor houses or bay-and-gable rowhouses from local brick. Their sons now had the means and leisure time to write new club charters, bylaws, and regulations, and to organize races and regattas.

Queen City Yacht Club was formed and inaugurated remarkably quickly, even before the club had a permanent home, funds, or furniture. Even though there were already two other yacht clubs in a city with a population of only 150,000, a group of sailors and active racers felt there was room for a smaller-class yacht club. They began discussing their plans and picking names in 1888. In the club archives, I come across a short 1903 article on "Club Life in Toronto," pasted into a yellowing scrapbook without the name of the publication or author, which reads: "in the early spring of 1889, a number of small boat-owners...held a meeting for the purpose of considering the advisability of organizing a yacht club to look after more particularly small boat and yacht racing in Toronto, as it was felt that the two clubs then in existence were devoting all their time and energies to larger classes, to the exclusion of the smaller." The wish for a club to represent the interests of small boat owners might have been enough motivation to found one, but I wonder if there were other common interests that also brought them together.

Present-day members explained to me that Queen City started as a "working man's club," as opposed to a club catering to Toronto's upper crust. Whatever the reason, it was enough for the founding members to formally launch the club and hold elections a few months later in July. Its first officers were Commodore Thomas A. E. World, Vice-Commodore W. McGill, Captain W. H. Clindinning, as well as a secretary, treasurer, measurer, and committees for executive, sailing, and house. The rapid coordination shows the level of commitment and enthusiasm among members. QCYC's volunteer officer and committee structure remain remarkably similar today.

Much has been written about the club's first commodore, Thomas World, who worked in finance and also owned a nearby boathouse. He had a reputation for being a capable organizer and extremely devoted to sailing, and was later a president of LYRA. In photographs, he has keen eyes and sports a very fine moustache. At the club's first meeting, Tommy was only twenty-seven. His friend William Clindinning was only twenty-two but was already married and working as a carpenter in his father's boat-building business. William's father, John, had built one of the new island ferry boats. Another member was Richard Slee, the great-grandfather of the present-day member. An engraver by trade, Richard had arrived in Toronto in 1890 and joined the club soon after—on his birthday, in fact—and later owned and raced *Caprice,* a locally built sixteen-foot gaff-rigged skiff. I can look up the addresses of all these early members in the *Toronto City Directory*, along with birth and death certificates. They bear surnames such as Allen, Imandt, Thomas, Haight, Lee, Riley, Ward, Dodd, and Foy—good Old Country Protestant names—and their given names are strings of Williams, Georges, Henrys, Johns, and Alexanders, making them as tricky to locate in the archives as a back-alley entrance.

"The club flourished during the next two or three years," the article continues, "and the membership increased rapidly, and it was not long before the Queen City Yacht Club was known from one end of the lake to the other as a most progressive institution and the home and school of some of the best sailors that Canada has ever turned out. This reputation, which the club gained in its infancy, it still retains, and gives ample proof from season to season of its right to do so." The new club was also quick to establish its visual identity in its first year by choosing the club colours of blue and gold horizontal stripes (the same colours used by RCYC), a unique club burgee flag, and ensign, the red Canadian ensign with a gold leaf. Lilley details that the club "quickly acquired accoutrements considered essential to a club of substance: pictures for its walls, a chandelier, subscriptions to Toronto's *The World* newspaper and the magazine *Forest and Stream*, a dozen chairs – eight plain at 65¢ each and four rockers at 75¢." With three floors that included a dinghy storage area, assembly room, ladies' room, offices, a veranda that wrapped around two sides, and attic living quarters for the steward, the south boathouse on Clindinning Row was a "commodious clubhouse situated in one of the most advantageous positions on the Bay," states the 1903 article. By the end of its first year, the club had expanded into two more adjoining boathouses, begun renovations on the club rooms above the boat storage, and hired a caretaker.

I'm getting a picture of a club made up of active working men who married young. Some had their own family trades and legacies, and expectations from their fathers. Some led itinerant lives. Others were restlessly searching for opportunities, new careers, and, of course, more occasions to sail and race. These were also men who recognized the need to draft constitutions and documents, forming processes and establishing a club identity through colours and ensigns. They were likely hardy and fit as spruce trees, due to the demands of racing skiffs that carried a lot of sail. They aren't my forefathers, so I don't feel much attachment to them, though I'm curious as to how they would react to Queen City's evolution. I would've loved to sit down with them over a pint of ale to hear about their first regatta and the cash prizes offered, as Lilley reveals that "some winners are on record complaining that prizes were too small to cover expenses of boat purchase and upkeep." I wonder what these earliest members would say if they knew that clubs no longer give any monetary rewards. Or that publications such as *Daily Mail and Empire*, the *Toronto World*, the *Evening Star,* and the *New York Times* no longer report on club business, race results, or regattas.

The only thing I can be certain about is that they wouldn't have been indifferent about the racing prizes or the diminishment of the public's interest in sailing events. All the sailors I know hold multifarious opinions on issues regarding sailing, racing, the club, and its community. That tendency has outlasted the nineteenth-century boathouses. Hanging out at the boat lockers is another club tradition still practised today. Perhaps traditions are stories we tell ourselves, not just about where we've been, but about where we're heading.

Like many Toronto tenants, QCYC searched for a permanent residence it could afford. The members initially rented out three boathouses on Clindinning Row for $140 a year. A few years later, in 1891, a special committee was formed to discuss a possible new clubhouse, but they couldn't locate any suitable grounds, nor was the club able to afford a purchase. Instead, they leased their current location, their rent leaping to $250 a year. In return for this steep rent hike, their landlords added new doors and a floating platform for launching boats. QCYC Ltd. was originally incorporated in August 1889 under the City of Toronto. Richard informed me that at the turn of the last century, establishing a social club and a corporation that held assets and issued shares was a popular move among gentlemen of the day. He also explained that some members served on both the club and the City of Toronto boards, leading to "some interesting arguments about who was going to fix the assets!" Despite the organization's working-class reputation, some Queen City board members held considerable power and influence, which they might've used to benefit the club.

I recall the harried, homeless feeling I had when I'd stored my worldly belongings in my uncle's basement while apartment hunting. Perhaps Queen City's members felt similarly when they deposited the club furniture into storage at 42 Church Street before leasing a new building owned by the Argonaut Boat Co. at the foot of York Street for $200 a year. With space rented on the Argonaut Pier, just north of the Toronto Canoe Club, a new three-storey building (costing $2,000) celebrated its opening in August 1902. It was designed by architect and club member E. J. Lennox, who also designed Casa Loma, Toronto's Old City Hall, the Bank of Toronto, and many other iconic Toronto buildings in the distinctly ornate Richardsonian Romanesque style. From its beginnings, QCYC drew on the varied talents of its members.

The squarish wooden building with an upper-floor balcony and a residence for the steward on the third floor looks simpler than Lennox's institutional buildings. Lennox was well-known for combining different architectural styles, and the new QCYC clubhouse had a Queen Anne–style sense of functionality and stateliness. A photo shows its balcony packed with Edwardian ladies in wide-brimmed hats and a row of spectators in dark suits and straw boater hats, their backs to the photographer as they watch a swimming event. Skiffs with half-raised mainsails are nestled along the side of the clubhouse, where more members perch, and in the distance double-handed dinghies pass alongside the hazy outline of a passenger vessel. The scene is energetic and amusing, and you can almost hear the joking commentary and feel the sun on woollen backs.

This handsome clubhouse wasn't destined to last. A few years before the outbreak of First World War, the Toronto Harbour Commission saw the need for an expanded waterfront with more land between the rail lines, and dock walls for the larger commercial ships that it anticipated, rather than a mishmash of wharves. It forcibly encouraged recreational clubs and organizations to relocate to lands near the Western Gap, offering QCYC thousands of dollars to move. But Tommy World preferred the location of Toronto Island, and the club put off a decision. By 1920, dredging operations were underway, removing sand from the middle of the harbour to create deeper ports and infill the shoreline. As well, Ashbridge's Bay marsh was reclaimed, and 650 acres of new land was set to be created on Toronto Island. QCYC members had connected with the Ward's Island Association to gain support and decided to move the club to the then-named Sunfish Island, hoping to float the clubhouse across.

Those hopes crashed into the harbour when a piling beneath the clubhouse collapsed one July afternoon in 1920. Dredging had destabilized the harbour bottom, and as a result the clubhouse's first storey tipped into the harbour. In photos, the wooden roof is intact but askew, and one corner of the frame leans into the harbour, as if the clubhouse was about to go for a swim. The noise of the crash and sound of the water rushing into the first-floor windows must've shocked the steward and his family, who managed to escape. The piano and club trophies were saved, but the clubhouse itself was later scrapped. Torontonians read about the disaster in the July 8 issue of the *Toronto Daily Star*. *QUEEN CITY YACHT CLUB COLLAPSES*, reads the headline, and a brief article follows: "The Star photographer shows the wrecked building of the Q.C.Y.C., foot of York Street, which collapsed yesterday owing to the rotting of the old wooden crib-work underneath it. The boats and dinghies in the north end of the structure are now under water. No one was hurt, although the steward, E. Simpkins, was in the building at the time and had to escape through an upper window." The club reached an out-of-court settlement that was used to fund its new clubhouse on Sunfish Island. This long spit had been expanded into Algonquin Island using sand dredged from the harbour bottom. Toronto's land reclamation projects had caused QCYC to lose one home and to gain a new one.

Contemplating the labour required to fill in the narrow spit with dredged harbour sands, to transport timber and brick to the island, to draft blueprints and to raise funds for a new clubhouse, I'm both admiring and critical. I want to acknowledge the will, determination, and hard work of those who built structures still used today, while disapproving of the colonial attitudes behind claiming terra nullius and ignoring the significance of the islands to Indigenous peoples, in particular the Mississauga, the Chippawa, and the Seneca Nations. I want to write this history in a way that is not mythic and that does not revere "founding fathers" but recognizes how the values of settlers and immigrants have shaped Toronto and its organizations. If the rise and fall of various QCYC clubhouses is seen as a manifestation of the city's character, I would describe it as determined, dramatic, resourceful, thrifty, indecisive, privileged, visionary, and parochial.

In its search for a permanent clubhouse, the club founders and builders irreversibly changed the landscape. There are certain kinds of human settlement that eradicate and alter natural spaces, and building a home is both constructive and destructive. The upper veranda of the current QCYC clubhouse is one of my favourite places to be in the city, especially when the tawny sunset makes the chipped walls glow. When I look out at the water skimmed with waterfowl and returning dinghies, my attachment to the club and my feelings of comfort make it hard for me to feel a sense of loss. Every view contains vanished edges. I want to be able to hold the present and the absent past, because I need both to locate myself and to be at home.

I have rented four different houses in Toronto. The first was a shared house near Ossington and Bloor on Concord Avenue dubbed "the Pentacon" for the five roommates who lived there. We loved it for its big table for "family dinners" and board game nights, its jam room, its upstairs patio, its sloping ceilings. When the owner's family decided to sell, Mark, Joe, Stephanie, Jenna, and I thought we'd never find a house that would suit us again, especially since by then we had a sixth roommate, Mark's brother Kirk, camping out in the music room. But we did find one—a many-roomed, three-floor house with a wide front porch on Broadview looking across the slopes of Riverdale Park East. It had hardwood floors, leaded glass-paned windows, a backyard deck, and a library with built-in shelves and a window seat. Our beds, couches, and dining table perfectly fit the myriad rooms. I've lived in a clean, two-bedroom basement in a bungalow a short walk from the Humber River. I furnished it with my roommates' hand-me-downs, curbside finds, and used furniture from Kijiji. It was an apartment that served as a resting space amidst my frenetic schedule until the pandemic descended, when I started to feel like I was living in a well-stocked bunker. I currently occupy a house on Symington, which is noisier than any other street I've lived on, but the house has high ceilings and good light. The owner hasn't given it the care it deserves, but I can make up for these deficiencies with philodendrons and pilea, and by replacing the gross, yellowy bathroom cabinet with a big mirror. I buy real adult furniture, yet I still feel a sense of impermanence. I'm tired of renting and want to own something of my own, but neither do I trust that desire. I worry that it's a capitalistic trap, an empty promise that could erode into silt.

Members ferrying over the harbour for their first meeting at the new clubhouse in July 1921 would've first seen a long, utilitarian building perched at the edge of Sunfish Island. For fifteen cents, Toronto Ferry Co. would drop passengers on Ward's Island, where they would whistle for a rowboat, as the bridge across the lagoon wasn't built until 1938. A row of white locker doors faced the harbour, opening to dinghy boat storage. Above, a balcony extended from the double doors that admitted fresh air into the Great Hall and stewards' quarters. In later photographs, QCYC is emblazoned on the low-pitched roof. The entrance on the building's south elevation faced a sandy spit, and images from the early 1920s and 1930s show young trees lining the lagoon. The grounds are unadorned of the paraphernalia I'm familiar with, the hull of *Rapids Queen* that acts as a breakwater next to the clubhouse has not yet been installed, and the lagoon is empty of the docks and rubber tire moorings.

The building was designed by architect and club member J. A. Mackenzie, and according to the labour and materials specifications he submitted to the club for what he called the "Construction of a Boat House and Dancing Pavilion for the Queen City Yacht Club at Sunfish Island," hemlock was used for the rafters, floors, roof, and exterior sheeting, and Douglas fir for posts, beams, braces, and sills, at a total cost of $19,250. As Lilley reports, the land was leased from the city for $100 a year plus taxes. Since then, this amount has ballooned to over $3,000 per acre per year, and it continues to increase with inflation. Though it's unlikely that the City of Toronto would ever cancel the lease agreement with QCYC, I also wouldn't approve of the club owning the land outright. The marginal sense of precarity that comes with being a tenant serves as a reminder that some places should not be possessed by one owner or disposed of as they see fit.

Inevitably, conversations among Torontonians turn to real estate, which I dread and relish at the same time. Mark, Quentin, Amanda, and I were on *Panache* for the Ashbridge's Bay Yacht Club Open coastal race one Sunday in May. We motored past the outer harbour and around Tommy Thompson Park, shutting off the engine across from the handsome R. C. Harris Water Treatment Plant. There wasn't enough wind to start the race. There had been no wind the previous day either. I felt bad that the race organizers had spent so much time to host the weekend, but there was nothing anyone could do. For four hours, we perched in the cockpit until hunger and thirst nudged us to chew on our sandwiches and crack open beers.

Mark started a speech about how he and his girlfriend, Sarah, would never be able to find another apartment to fit their budget if they had to move. Quentin expressed regret that he hadn't bought an apartment when he first moved to Toronto and offers his opinion on the overinflated prices of condos. Amanda brought up the advantages and disadvantages of fixed versus variable mortgage rates and shared that she'd bought a condo in Victoria that she was currently renting out. Since shortly after grad school, she's lived in the same bachelor apartment, and similar units currently go for double what she pays. I mention that my dad has been urging me to "build equity," and I share my recently acquired knowledge about second mortgage programs. No one has trapped us here in Toronto, but we feel unable to move.

After the members refused the Toronto Harbour Commission's offer to lease three hundred feet for $1,500 near the Western Gap at the bottom of Bathurst Street, they waited throughout the rest of 1920 for the commission's out-of-court settlement. The club was tight on cash until they received the payment of $15,000. Broker and commodore Tommy World, along with another club member, Blake Van Winkle, arranged for the clubhouse contractor to take back a five-year mortgage at 6 percent interest, payable at $400 a year. I believe this is what is known as a vendor take-back mortgage, a type of loan where the seller extends a loan to the buyer to secure the property's sale, thereby benefiting both the buyer and the seller. However, I've never heard of a contractor profiting this way—it sounds dubious to me. These and other machinations were required to finance Queen City's clubhouse on Algonquin Island in 1921.

The board also drafted a new charter to allow for the sale of shares at $50 each and bonds issued at $25 each. Apparently, the rush to build the clubhouse came partly from Tommy's fear that they would lose members if building was delayed.

Fortunately, the settlement came through and the club had a bit of financial stability. In 1921, the club was incorporated with letters patent under Ontario provincial law, which declares that the club will be "carried on without the purpose of gain for its members, and any profits or other accretions to the Corporation shall be used in promoting its objects," which were primarily to encourage and promote yacht, skiff, and canoe sailing. A century ago, the club's leadership and board members had to use creative machinations to finance their new home. I have a feeling if they could hear us today, moaning about current mortgage rates and house prices, they'd disgustedly tell us to pull ourselves up by our bootstraps and hustle. Times have changed, and I'm relieved that the club no longer has to resort to fantastic fundraising schemes. Though without the determined actions of Tommy World and other past board members, the club wouldn't have survived, so who am I to criticize?

The lagoon in February is a plate of bubbled glass, with twigs, sandwich wrappers, and plastic bags trapped in the ice near the pilings. I've never come to QCYC in the winter when the slips are empty and the boats are sleeping under their tarps. Amanda, Sue, and I take the open-decked *Ongiara* ferry to Ward's Island in our puffy jackets and toques for the unveiling of the club's renovated snug and a Groundhog Day party. As house chair for several years, Mark has led these renovation efforts, and he spent weekends with a volunteer crew removing and rebuilding the snug's ceiling, installing raccoon-resistant bulkheads, sprayfoaming and installing insulation, adding a firebreak, air conditioning, and audiovisual technology for webconferencing in the boardroom, and many more unglamorous but necessary repairs and upgrades to the hundred-year-old building. I admire the recessed lighting and new furnishings in the snug and adjoining boardroom. Club paraphernalia, paintings, and photos are pieces of the colourful past on the newly painted walls.

As if reading from a list tacked onto the walls of his mind, Mark tells me that the roof, the north end of the balcony, the Great Hall windows, and the doors are leaking in several places. The staircase has been a sore spot for members concerned with what they can see, and the railings have already been redone but the carpet needs replacing. The outer white siding is damaged, though neither of us can understand what might have caused this—gulls colliding into it? Members ramming masts into the surface? The cement-based siding product he requires for the repair is manufactured in Texas and is only available in the US. Members come to him with constant house-related complaints. I begin stockpiling complaints of my own to harass him with—the need for an accessibility ramp, charging stations, a sauna and pool.

Despite my teasing, I know what it's like to have a never-ending to-do list and I'm sympathetic. Being house chair means giving up the luxury of seeing the clubhouse as someone else's responsibility. I imagine it's like being imbued with X-ray vision, which might seem like a superpower but is more like a burden. I wonder if Mark worries over the clubhouse's permeability to rain, rot, and wildlife, and its degrading wiring, plumbing, and foundations, every time he looks at its beams and posts. However, there are rewards too, such as the satisfaction of witnessing guests and members laughing under the Great Hall rafters, of running fingers over slick banisters, and the indefinite value of contributing to a legacy. I have seen actions and decisions enter the archive: the construction of the marine railway, the design of a new club badge, or the repainting of the junior clubhouse. Sometimes names are recorded, sometimes they are not. Some names peel off like old event posters, some have other names glued over them, under layers of insultation and plaster, so faint I can hardly make them out.

Excavated pits dot downtown Toronto like a giant's pockmarks. I pause at chain-link fences, peering down several storeys to where the CAT cranes rake silt and sand into mini-mountains. The perimeter of the construction site is lined with ostentatious images of towers with twisted spines. Each year when I walk from Union Station, past the SkyDome, down York Street, and under the Gardiner, there seems to be another new spire along the lakeshore. My friends share stories of "ghost hotels" and draconian condo boards. A north wind will travel through the corridors of Yonge and University, producing gusts on the harbour, as though the city were exhaling. In Hong Kong, buildings and apartments have spaces and holes constructed into their facades, gates for the spirit dragons that travel from the hills down to the water. Blocking their paths is considered bad feng shui, and I wonder if Toronto's palisade of condos might bring misfortune to the city.

In July 2014, while digging for the foundations of the Tridel condo tower at 10 York Street, the excavator bucket's teeth scraped against buried timber. As they lifted out the sediment, a long crib of greyish, squared logs was exposed to light and air for the first time in nearly a century. Craig White, a writer and editor at *Urban Toronto*, identifies it as Tinning's Wharf, built by Richard Tinning in the 1830s at the bottom of York Street on the city's original shoreline. However, Richard Slee notes that on an 1857 map, Tinning's Wharf is slightly to the east of York Street, and he believes the excavation instead uncovered the Argonaut Rowing Club wharf, on which the 1902 Queen City clubhouse was situated. I've read that Tinning's Wharf was bought and demolished by CP Rail in 1886, and I cannot find it on any archived Toronto map after that date. History is an approximation, but I have located something more than just photographs, dredged harbour silt, and crushed cellulose. This is as close as I can get to an irrecoverable address. When I walk down to the shore, I know exactly where I am.

In Pursuit

UNAUTHORIZED SAILING INSTRUCTIONS

1.   RULES
1.1   I don't know why I said yes. I'd heard around the club
        that the position needed to be filled, so six weeks be-
        fore the event, I volunteered to chair the Women's
        Open Regatta. As a new associate member, I had ben-
        efited from others' organization of races and regattas
        for years. I had a vague sense of owing something.
1.2   I heard a professor speak about a system that she
        and two close academic friends had instituted in or-
        der to avoid overcommitting. Any time one of them
        was considering taking on another role or project,
        they required the approval of the other two. They
        assigned quotas to various types of commitments,
        such as mentoring or editing an anthology, and once
        they were used up, they were not allowed to say yes
        to anything else for the rest of the year.

1.3   I suggested this system to the two closest friends I'd made in grad school: Joanne, originally from Singapore, an academic and a creative writer, and Amanda, a Tamil-Canadian from Victoria who works in health policy and government relations. All three of us, like many working women in their forties, cycle through exhaustion, burnout, and recovery. But I know I can't solely rely on the women in my life to hold me accountable.

2.   CHANGES TO SAILING INSTRUCTIONS

2.1   Even at QCYC, one of the most welcoming clubs for women, I can count the number of female skippers in Wednesday-night races on one hand. Plenty of boats have female crew, and women jointly own boats and sail them on cruises, but invariably, the names of skippers in most sailing races and regattas are male. I don't know what can be done to change this lack of gender equality in sailing. Or, I do know what can be done and feel I lack capacity to undertake it. The work feels insurmountable, and changes will come about so slowly that I'll grow frustrated.

2.2   I admit I wasn't aware of what had already been done by others to remedy the lack of equality and representation. I looked for models in the numerous clubs that have women's sailing and racing programs, such as Kingston Yacht Club's Women in Wind, which is aimed at building racing and dinghy sailing skills. Since 1982, the women of the club have organized seamanship instruction and weeknight sails. One of the former co-chairs of the program explained what inspired the program: as a social norm, male boat owners weren't allowing their wives to helm their own boats, and this caused concern among women. If their husbands had a heart attack or another crisis out on the water, they wouldn't be able to reach help. The program more than fulfilled its intention, as she emailed me: "There were several experienced sailors who took other female members out on their boats and taught them how to sail their own boats. No men allowed. I think the women had a ball. They got to the point where they would take the boats out for overnights and left their partners behind on the dock with binoculars."

3.   COMMUNICATIONS WITH COMPETITORS

3.1   A Queen City member in his eighties said to me that women lack the ego to be competitive racers. Though I have no wish to helm a boat over a hectic start line or order around a crew, I know women who are just as intent on winning as male racers, maybe more so. Perhaps my lack of desire is influenced by racing's sometimes aggressive atmosphere. There are skippers who hate losing, but not all men race to satisfy their ego and vanity. Many value respect, teamwork, and building the confidence of their crew. Perhaps women like myself would be more likely to race if the conditions, values, and tone of the races reflected what we hold to be important: co-operation, creativity, and problem-solving. What would a collaborative and supportive racing event look like? What does it mean to race with intuition, sensitivity, and wisdom? Have those characteristics always been present but not emphasized or acknowledged?

4.   CODE OF CONDUCT

4.1   I had been told by my female friends learning to sail at their dinghy clubs about male members who, acting as mentors, made women feel uncomfortable. Who touched women without their consent, and when those women complained, it was to volunteer boards who did little more than have private conversations with the men. Who did not revoke memberships, or ban the men from their clubs, or encourage members to sign up for anti-sexism and harassment workshops, or adopt anti-gender discrimination and equity-based policies. Who failed to protect these women.

4.2   I've read stories about women who signed up to cruise with male boat owners and/or skippers who made unwanted advances and also contrived to make it extremely difficult for the women to disembark. I have heard the argument that boats are private property, and so clubs and sailing organizations are absolved from being responsible for what takes place on board. That it isn't their job to enforce respectful behaviour among their members, and, in fact, they would have difficulty doing so.

4.3   I have never been subject to anything worse than a few patronizing comments from male members at the club, or assumptions that I was someone's girlfriend and not an active crew member. I've also had the feeling that this domineering manner was applied to everyone, regardless of gender. The majority of men I meet in the sailing community are kind, respectful, and considerate. This might imply that a code of conduct around sexism, discrimination, or violence is unnecessary in yacht clubs and communities. Indeed, I have my doubts about the value of the language in codes of conduct, because they can be lip service or token gestures if there are no actions to back them up. I have my doubts that language is enough.

5. SCHEDULE OF RACES

5.1 My schedule was always full, but now it became difficult to finish all my regatta organizing tasks within days and weeks—or the month I had. I began drafting a donor letter to send to local breweries and to prize sponsors, sending poster copy to a volunteer designer for a new logo and poster, emailing possible performers and bands for the after-party, sourcing quotes for regatta hats and shirts, promoting the regatta at our club and at clubs in the area, coordinating a team of volunteers that included Amanda, Jade, Tala, Teresa, Beth, and Robin, and myriad other tasks. There was always another email to write, another task to check off. At some point I realized that whatever was left undone would probably not be missed, or could wait.

6. RACING AREA

6.1 My mother is the oldest sibling, with four younger brothers. Even when she became a teenager and started to wear miniskirts and to date, in her heart she was still a tomboy, with an air of island wildness about her. When my sister and I were growing up, my mother shopped for us in the boys' section: we wore jean overalls and navy sweaters. My sister was often mistaken for a boy, with her skinny hips and short hair. When my dad needed someone to hold a clamp or to help with moving furniture, it made no difference if I was his son or daughter. I wasn't catcalled or bothered after seeing a show in Vancouver's Downtown Eastside if I dressed in jeans, Converse sneakers, and a hoodie. I have never thought of myself as a tomboy—my hips are too wide, I have a too bookish and innocent air. The older I get, the more I resemble my mother, with her uniform of jeans and T-shirts, her taste for minimalism, her resistance to any labels except that of a human.

7.   COURSES

7.1   The course selected to be sailed will be announced at the participants' meeting and will also be displayed on a sign at the stern of the race committee signal vessel no later than thirty minutes before the first scheduled start time. Also, the race committee may make periodic radio courtesy announcements from the time of posting until after the last scheduled start.

7.2   Short course, four nautical miles: Promote the Women's Open Regatta as widely as possible. Encourage female skippers to sign up. Choose the pursuit race format where each boat has its own start time adjusted to its PHRF, which is more accommodating for less experienced skippers.

7.3   Medium course, seven nautical miles: Ask members to record videos on what gender equality means to them for the club social media. Hold an info session on the pursuit race format and strategies, and/or record a presentation about pursuit race strategies. Encourage girls from the learn-to-sail program to crew with a female skipper.

7.4   Long course, ten nautical miles: Set up a women's mentoring sailing program. Record interviews with women in the club and archive them for future generations. Hold an annual count of female board members, boat owners, skippers, and crew, and set targets. Facilitate a workshop session with Canadian Women & Sport on retaining women in sport. Organize a dedicated casual women's race night.

8.   MARKS
8.1   How will we know that gender equality in sailing has been achieved? When women make up 50 percent or more of club members? Of board members? Of senior members? Numbers reveal a lot that even stories cannot. What are our benchmarks? What are our goals? Are they actionable?

9.   OBSTRUCTIONS
9.1   There will always be people who exclaim, "You sail?" and I will always read too much into their arched brows of disbelief.
9.2   There will always be people who ask me what I'm complaining about. Who will question the need for a women's skipper race and make me question it as well.

9.3   There will always be older men who correct me even though I know I'm right, and I will press my lips and nod.

9.4   Even younger men, men my own age, men I trust and joke around with, tell me things I already know. Maybe they honestly don't think I know. Because how much do we know, really, about what other people contain? I forgive them. I acknowledge the giant chip on my shoulder. I ignore that weird, pontificating tone of voice these men use, like they are possessed by the spirits of their dads and uncles and grandfathers. Maybe it's this tone of voice that enables them to take up space in a world of hierarchies and rigid structures and other pontificating men.

9.5   There is danger in binary thinking because it is reductive and does not allow for categories to be fluid, overlapping, and messy. People can be both masculine and feminine, empathetic and selfish, confident and insecure, dangerous in their very harmlessness, in their unwillingness to think dangerously.

10.   THE START

10.1 The root of the problem was that I chronically overcommitted myself. I had no understanding of my limits. I have always done more than what was expected of me, and I no longer know what a reasonable amount of work is. My body doesn't know either. I've had decades of practice ignoring pain and discomfort. I intertwined acts of service with my identity so that to say "no" means to reject the part of myself that I thought earned me the most love and approval.

11.   THE FINISH

11.1   The finish is between the blue flag on the race com-
       mittee signal vessel and the horizon.

11.2   The finish is nearby.

11.3   There is no finish line.

12.   TIME LIMIT AND TARGET TIMES

12.1   There was only so much I could do in the four weeks
       leading up to the regatta. The organizing team and
       I secured ten flats of non-alcoholic beverages from
       Collective Arts. After the race, a keg of Great Lakes
       Ale showed up unannounced from the club restau-
       rant. There were gift cards, beer glasses, and beer
       packs from local breweries, donated summer reads
       from both my publishers, and Gil duffle bags donat-
       ed by Carolyn at the Rigging Shoppe. I asked a friend
       and fellow poet, Jessica Moore, to play her delicate
       songs on the lawn, accompanied by Degan Davis on
       keyboards. Beth and I bought feathers and ribbons
       and sparkle glue, which we set up for lantern- and
       mask-making on the picnic tables. We could've done
       more if we'd had more time.

13.   HEARING REQUESTS

13.1   On the lawn after the race, without a microphone,
       I addressed the racers and thanked them for partic-
       ipating. I spoke of the women who had supported
       me at the club with advice, humour, stories, and
       mentoring. I acknowledged the mothers, grand-
       mothers, aunties, and Indigenous caretakers of this
       land, the Missisaugas of the Credit, who had named

the islands Mnisiing and viewed them as a place of healing. I spoke of the work still to be done toward pursuing gender equality in sailing. I did not use the word *redress*. I did not use the word *protest*. I hoped that the ancestors had heard me. Afterwards, someone told me he was impressed that I hadn't needed any notes for my speech.

14.   SCORING

14.1   In a pursuit race, everyone should finish at the same time. The slowest-rated boat starts first and needs to block faster boats from passing them, and the faster boats have to overtake those ahead of them. Of course, in practice, not all boats will complete the race at the same time. Different wind conditions, tactics, and the capabilities of the skippers and crew are factors. Certain wind conditions favour certain types of boats.

14.2   During the race, I had little to do on *Panache*, with Amanda on the helm, Mark as tactician, and Jade and Tala trimming sails. Because of the wind direction and the L-shaped course, going from south of the Toronto Islands east toward the Gibraltar buoy and then northwest to the Dufferin buoy in Humber Bay, we sailed upwind or on reaches. Mark believes *Panache* is fastest downwind, but we hadn't had a true downwind so I hadn't needed to put up the pole. Still, we did well, finishing eighth overall and second in our fleet. It was a gorgeous day for a sail, light saturating our tank tops, and I leaned against the mast after a hectic morning of transporting drinks and preparing for the participants meeting. Later, discussing the race with Amanda, I wondered aloud if bearing off would have had us sailing faster than constantly adjusting the course to sail slightly high of the mark, and she disagreed, saying that it would have required a longer distance. I didn't mind being corrected. Amanda and I have been friends a long time. We don't keep score.

15.   SAFETY REGULATIONS

15.1   This is not, nor has it ever been, a safe space. If you choose to retire early, please notify the race committee at the first reasonable opportunity on the assigned radio channel.

16.   PRIZES

16.1   I searched everywhere for sailing stories written by women I could identify with. I'm still searching for the sailing book I wish I could've read when I first started. I have found books on swimming to inspire me, such as Jessica Lee's *Turning*, Leanne Shapton's playfully illustrated *Swimming Studies*, and Bonnie Tsui's *How We Swim*. I loved a *New York Times* article on poet Wang Ping's rowing workout and my friend Joanne Leow's long-form essay on her jiu jitsu practice. I remember when the late Priscila Uppal was the poet-in-residence for Canadian Athletes Now during the 2010 Vancouver Olympics. There are many essays and memoirs written by Asian-Canadian women on topics such as race, family, food, culture, and education. I know there are writers who learned how to helm an Optimist as a kid at camp or who've gone for an evening sunset sail, but I don't know who they are. For those who haven't, it dismays me to think that they've never known the pleasure of feeling a boat heel and pick up speed. And the women of colour I do know in the sailing community haven't shared or written their stories, at least not yet. They haven't been asked for their stories. Perhaps I'm writing this book to find them. That would be my biggest prize.

17.   RISK STATEMENT

17.1   Rule three of the Racing Rules of Sailing states: 'The responsibility for a boat's decision to participate in a race or to continue to race is hers alone.' By participating in this event, each competitor agrees and acknowledges that sailing is a potentially dangerous activity with inherent risks. These risks include strong winds and rough seas, sudden changes in weather, failure of equipment, boat-handling errors, poor seamanship by other boats, loss of balance on an unstable platform, and fatigue, resulting in increased risk of injury. Inherent in the sport of sailing is the risk of permanent, catastrophic injury or death by drowning, trauma, hypothermia, or other causes.

18.   INSURANCE

18.1   Sometimes other older women are tougher on me than men. I'm corrected and criticized while my male crewmates sit beside me, blithely unaware. It's a painful manifestation of inequality, a double standard that is worse than being underestimated by men. I need more emotional insurance against other women's judgments, though they reveal more about their own exigencies than mine. I need to protect myself against unexpected damage due to weather, accident, theft, collisions, and loss. For those damages and losses I have already sustained, I must seek to recoup what I am owed. The full value may never be recovered, due to depreciation and other factors, and I have always understood this risk.

The Summer of
Endless Fun, Part 2

As if slowly waking from a nap, the trees stretch their bare
arms overhead. It's April and the day isn't waiting for anything
anymore. The yard is faint with noises, ladders creaking, a few
nonsensical birds. I've been using a drill to remove nails from
some wooden props and donkeys Mark no longer wants to
use. We've applied a thin layer of copper paint to *Panache*'s
bottom, followed by a coat of wax. Now we're eating lunch
by the lockers with Paul and a couple of older members. I
take a piece of paper from my knapsack and slide it to Mark
with a pen. His eyes crinkle when he recognizes what it is.
"This is historic," he says. I pass it to Paul next, who signs
without hesitation. It's the start of my fourteenth season sailing at Queen City. I walk to the office to hand in my application form for associate membership, feeling chuffed that it
was so easy to find two senior members to endorse my application. The buds above me swell, about to burst.

Fog has sealed the harbour, and from the stern deck of the *Algonquin Queen,* we watch island water taxis, sailboats, and the long wooden navy-hulled Royal Canadian club tender, *Kwasind,* slip in and out of the mist like premonitions. We'll be on island time soon. When I get to the club, I hear talk that the review of the fleet is cancelled because of the fog. I've always found fog immensely comforting, and creative in a way. The high-rises behind us have vanished into white clothing, and the harbour is filled with other possibilities.

I show up for Sailpast without an invitation from any of the skippers I know, not expecting to get out on a boat, but Mark waves me over. The fog is now clearing and the review of the fleet is back on. Sarah steps onto *Panache* while we ready the boat. I remind Mark to get the QCYC burgee flag up and take the helm while he hoists it. There's enough wind that the boat wants to heel, and instead of sailing close-hauled, which is my instinct, I remind myself we're not racing and bear off, flattening the boat so Sarah's more comfortable. Over the radio I hear the instruction that it's now our turn to sail past the commodore's boat. All the boats of the club are supposed to arrange themselves in order of smallest to biggest, but sometimes this is too much to manage. Mark takes the tiller and we head toward *Sansei,* where Jeffery Imai and his family, and other board members, are standing, grinning in their formal dress. We're not supposed to salute, only luff the jib as we pass. There are waves and cheers and our photograph is taken.

This ceremony has naval origins. British monarchs have reviewed the fleet since the time of Henry VIII. Many clubs around the lake also hold Sailpasts in late May. It's one of two times that I dress up at the club—the awards banquet being the other. The folds of my navy velvet skirt wrap between my legs as I flake the main and hook on the mooring lines. Afterwards, the commodore and senior board members motor into the lagoon on the pontoon boat, accompanied by bagpipes. As they pass the sterns of the boats in their slips, members blast airhorns that sound like raucous ducks. Later, at the club, we refill our punch cups until the afternoon becomes hazy with chit-chat. I don't stay for the formal dinner. There will be plenty more parties, and I have a feeling I ought to pace myself.

I push my fingertips into my ears as the gun bursts across the lagoons. They're just blanks, but the birds don't know that, and neither do the passengers on the Ward's Island ferry who turn and gape. The sharp retort from the three-foot cannon, which looks like a toy on the table, brings us back in time to when Fort York defended the city from the Americans. A small cloud of smoke appears as *Life Aquatic,* one of the new boats at the club, passes the bow of the *Rapids Queen* and I can smell the acrid gunpower while sitting on the clubhouse gallery balcony. *Life Aquatic* slows and Paul Horne reloads. It's a three-gun salute, the second gun firing as the boat passes the red buoy to the left, and the third firing as the boat enters the lagoon and everyone on the balcony cheers. I'm startled every time at the tearing noise of the cannon, wishing I'd brought earplugs. My adrenaline spikes and I help myself to the rum punch to calm my nerves. It's delicious, and vaguely dangerous.

The agenda for the New Members' Day & Night in early June is as follows:

13:00   Skippers meeting for all participants in the Great Hall

13:30   New member boats to motor out to the harbour

13:45   Gunning in of new member boats as they assemble in order for salute

14:00   Instructions via Channel 69 will indicate when you should enter the lagoon while members cheer and toast from the balcony

18:00   Party in the Great Hall to meet our new members with wine, food, and a dance with the Gibraltar Point band

19:30   Burgees and empty shells will be presented at New Members Night

I walk down to the brief edge of lawn to take a closer look at the cannon, fixed with a brass plate inscribed with the following:

Al Rae 1908–1977
A respected competitor, he carried the club burgee
to every port aboard his Tumlaren *Valhalla*. His name
graces many local and international trophies. A
driving force in the club, he served as commodore
many times. He became a legend in his own time.
His memory lives on in the club archives and in
the hearts of those who knew him.

I'm too young to have ever met Al Rae, but I know his son, Al Rae Jr., and his daughter, Justine. There are many spirits walking the grounds of this club. I imagine them hanging out by the lockers, glasses of punch in hand.

"Do you mind if I join you?"

An older woman sits down at my table and we introduce ourselves. Nancy tells me she buys a new boat every few years and has finally found one that she is comfortable with. She was gunned in for her first two boats but isn't eligible this year because she isn't a new member. But I later learn this isn't true, that a new member with a boat or a new boat belonging to an existing member can be gunned in.

"Is this unique to our club?" I ask Ron Mazza, who I expect would know. He does. It is. The three empty shells are given to the boat owner to keep as good-luck charms.

It's late June and the air is full of fluffies, bursting like confetti. It's warm and humid, and the trees are full of chartreuse promises. I wait for this colour all year. Below the balcony, Pat's pacing back and forth, giving directions on the radio to the new members coming into the lagoon, while Don Hinchley takes photographs. Dan Smith stands on the balcony in his grandfather's navy jacket. He calls down to one past commodore, his hand on his brow, "How long do I have to salute, like the whole time?"

"Do you want them to vote for you next year?"

There is Thomas and Elif on *Life Aquatic*, a Tanzer 26; Maisie and Liam on *The Antelope*, a J22; *Hour Time*, a C&C 27 owned by Rafel and Brechann; *Meridian*, a familiar red hull at QCYC with new owners, Neale and Alex; *Evelina*, owned by Christian and Robin; Karen and Evan on *Seraphina*, a Shark 24; Josh on *Caetera*, a Hinterholler 28; and finally, *Miss Kate*, a Catalina 34 owned by Fred and Ruth.

These are all just names to me. I don't know yet that Thomas will dress in lederhosen for an OcThomasfest birthday BBQ and that Elif will always give me an enormous smile when we meet. I haven't yet seen Rafel sail the QCYC Open Regatta single-handedly. Neale hasn't yet invited me and the rest of *Panache*'s crew to sail with him on his first race night. *Seraphina* hasn't yet won a flag in the Women's Open—which I don't yet know I'll be chairing. I have no idea that Josh and I will end up crewing together on *Amelia*, or that I will unintentionally embarrass him by telling Jade and Tala how he announces, "Helm's a-lee!" when tacking. I haven't even met Jade and Tala.

I already had plenty of friends, friends I hardly had time to see, friends to message about writing contracts and our parents' health and dating and our hectic work schedules. Nonetheless, I learn the names of these friendly faces at the club and they learn mine.

"Remember, by tradition, any skipper passing the clubhouse with fenders down will be obligated to buy drinks for any member who witnesses such a travesty!"

I don't recall who says this, but I take the warning seriously.

I write my name on a name tag and sip a glass of white wine in the Great Hall. New members get free wine all night, but that's not the only reason I'm here. We are called up and cheered at the front of the room, and have our hands shaken and photographs taken. I'm flattered by the volume of cheers when my name is called, because most of my crew aren't

here. Amanda shows up for the evening, and we uncharac-
teristically approach and introduce ourselves to the fresh new
faces on the balcony. We meet Thuyen, one of the owners of
the Runaway Cafe, which serves coffee and snacks from a vintage pink van in front of the Riviera restaurant on Algonquin
Island, just on the other side of the lagoon at Queen City. I'll
hear about her plans to buy a boat later in the summer when
I stop by for an Americano. Later, the senior members switch
name tags, and it's harmless, but why does everything at this
club turn into a giant inside joke?

After I pay my spring membership dues, I am sent a fifty-five-
page member handbook. I have wanted to get my hands on
this manual for years. I'm the type of person who reads the
guidebooks for new appliances and rules manuals for games.
I like having all the information in front of me for reference,
like board positions and the responsibilities of the various volunteer chairs, and where dinghies can be tied and dock boxes
can be installed. There are reminders of the "self-help" nature
of the club, the need for volunteer work, and repeated instructions to keep areas clean, tidy, and "ship-shape." The member
handbook contains answers to questions I didn't know I had.

Before joining, my source of information about the club
came from the website, the club's monthly *Clipper* magazine,
which is published from May until October, bulletin boards,
and word of mouth. After joining, I have access to the mem-
bers-only area of the website and receive the twice-weekly
e-newsletter, *Quick Clipper*, which only board members can
contribute to. I am added to the QChat, a Google chat forum.
There are at least several posts weekly, sometimes daily, with

reminders about Friday trivia nights organized by Leo and Christian, pickleball games, yoga, the chess club, free courses and performances and art openings around the island. Dave posts a picture of a lens cap I dropped on the lawn during one movie night, searching for its owner. Bruce asks if anyone has found his adjustable wrench and vice grips. It's even used to alert members when a child is separated from their parents. Josh and I agree that the QChat is worth the price of membership for its entertainment value alone. I use it to ask if any member has a canoe or kayak I can borrow for Flotilla Night. Within a few hours of posting, I get three offers.

I'm feeling anti-social, tired from volunteering that morning at PCYC on the race committee boat for the Lake Ontario 300. I stroll around Ward's Island to breathe in the quiet. Then I manoeuvre my way to the two long tables where Amanda and her friends from the St. James Town Sailing Club are sucking back oysters. Amanda offers me one briny swallow topped with lemon. A live band, the Circumstantialists, are strumming for hundreds of members, friends, and families. I've heard stories that QCYC's Lobsterfest has been called "the biggest party on the lake," with dozens of boats visiting, and to me, the club already feels full to bursting. Bottles of pinot grigio are pulled from knapsacks, and coolers of cold beer sit at our feet. Kids are halfway up a tree near the lockers with a circle of parents hovering below, and goldendoodles pull at their leashes. I can't finish my meal. I feel glutted with more than just lobster, potato salad, and corn. I tuck my remaining lobster into a Ziploc bag to go with my scrambled eggs, something else to look forward to.

Before this summer, I had ever only attended Sailpast, the awards banquet, and events after races and regattas. But now that I was obligated as an associate member to use up my "minimum spend," I bought tickets to QCYC's most famous smorgasbords. Essentially, members prepay for tickets when they pay their annual spring membership dues, and the amount is deducted for each ticketed event. "Club-mandated socializing," I call it. At these events, I meet many of the members who prefer cruising to racing. The club starts to feel like one of those reversible images where you either see a vase or two faces in profile, a young woman or an old one. I try to hold both views at the same time, but it's disorienting. There is something here for everyone. I'm not obligated to find one aspect of the club better than another, or even to have fun.

When I return to Toronto in July after two weeks of hiking and writing in BC, I wade through a deluge of work. I spend what little spare time I have at the club, neglecting festivals, literary events, seeing friends, and dating. I don't have to care for an elder or a child and yet I can barely manage to keep my apartment clean, shop for groceries, and exercise. For several years I've held a reputation among my friends and writing community for being constantly busy. I hate how this has become my identity, but to address the source of my over-work sounds like another project I don't have time for.

Seeing Jennifer, QCYC's entertainment chair, and her canoeing partner pushing off the dinghy ramp, I hurry over to Steve Hill's red kayak. "I'll be right there!" I call, collecting my beer from Mark's locker, stowing my dinner and knapsack in the bow hatch, and asking Nancy, who's passing by, to help me carry the vessel to the ramp. I catch up quickly, following Jennifer under the footbridge. A motley collection of canoes, kayaks, paddleboards, and dinghies pause near Snake Island, soaking in the view of the CN Tower and bank buildings and Harbourfront, saturated in pinks and golds. It's a short paddle, and about a dozen of us haul our watercraft against the steep bank and clamber up. I'm ravenous after an afternoon of swimming and regatta chair tasks, and I eat my dinner on a picnic table as the others photograph themselves against the sunset. A woman named Beth tells me she plans to help out at the Women's Open Regatta, that she doesn't like to race but prefers to work "behind the scenes." I thank her between bites of greasy chicken and rice. Later, I laugh as she pushes through the waterways while her partner, Keith, lounges in the bow of their canoe, taking photos. He later sends a few to me: in one, I'm dipping an oar to the side, making soft ripples behind me and looking like I know where I'm going.

Wednesday race nights had been my favourite night of the week. Why hadn't I calculated that spending more time at the club and on the island would increase my happiness? There were club members who had figured this out much earlier than I had. Arriving on a weekend with a long list of errands, such as dropping off receipts at the office, postering for the Women's Open Regatta, and interviewing members for book research is just a pretext for me to hop over to the island for a swim, sail, or paddle. What else would I do with a Saturday morning in July? There's always someone to have a beer with, and it takes me half an hour to walk from *Panache* to the clubhouse because I stop to say hello to members out for an afternoon sail with the kids, making boat repairs, and barbecuing afterwards. On weekends, there's chess club on the lawn, weddings in the clubhouse, boats heading out for a cruise. The perfect day is one that ends with me sinking easily into sleep after several hours of sun and water, like a fender dropped overboard.

It's the evening before the Women's Open and I don't plan to stay out late. Mark joins me at his table—he's playing singalong sea shanties and Stan Rogers covers with Dan Smith and a few other members. There's the usual Gordon Lightfoot, Joni Mitchell, and Bob Dylan covers. Valerie, who organized the open mic night, accompanies herself on the guitar while singing a Caribbean folk tune. A mother-and-daughter duo play a First Aid Kit cover. There's enough talent that the club could record and release an album: *Blow the Man Down* by the QCYC Singers. Or perhaps: *Songs from the QCYC Rolling Jib Chorus*.

I'm the only poet performing. I've read in many venues but never in the Great Hall. I choose two poems, the first based on a maritime painting by William Turner, *Sunrise with Sea Monsters*, and the other imagining Odysseus and Penelope when they are younger and out for an evening sail. It's the only poem I've written about sailing. I don't know why, since sailing is inherently poetic. Lyric poetry has its origins in song—it was first accompanied by the lyre. Our words and music drift out the windows, offerings for the club's hungry spirits.

August condenses. It brings out sweat and a shiny sheen on our skin, which mixes with our sunscreen. The trees are a mellow green. One week is sodden with humidity, another is brisk. When I walk across the lawn, August stretches my shadow.

Amanda S., JP, and I are attempting to manoeuvre an Ideal 18 out of the watery weeds beside the Royal Canadian Yacht Club's tender launch dock. We use the oar to push them off the rudder, giving a show to the diners on the clubhouse restaurant's balcony. I did well with steering the boat toward the lagoon after a few hours of shifty, petulant breeze in the lake, but had to slow to avoid *Kwasind* leaving the dock, and that's when we were pushed into the weeds. As RCYC members, Amanda S. and JP can sign out these club boats, which is a very appealing perk of their membership. I feel odd, even disloyal, to be sailing under their club flag. I don't hold it against the Ideal 18, which is so light and well-designed it can practically find the wind on its own, for suddenly heeling and powering up when we sail into a breezy patch. As we take turns practising on the helm, we discuss the new organization to promote diversity in sailing and encourage more Asian-Canadians to try the sport. After putting the boat away, we eat dinner on the very club patio I noticed from the water. I'm enthusiastic about the menu's variety and am told the new chef is Vietnamese, but this appreciation is offset by the realization that RCYC's minimum spend is much higher than my own club's. JP gives me a tour of the carpeted galleries, the painted ceilings in the rooms that feel like they could stage a debutante ball, the Arts and Crafts buildings, and the grounds. I praise everything I see. When JP buzzes me out of the gate, I bike through the dusk and wet grass back to Algonquin Island, splendid in its peace.

"Get back from there!" a senior member admonishes me.

I lower my little Olympus Pen camera and step back from the two pigs rotating on a spit under a tent by the clubhouse. There's something primal and ancient about raw meat cooked outdoors. In a couple of clear plastic bags, I see the shapes of pig parts that won't be cooked. Perhaps they will be offerings to the gods of summer feasting.

I feel guilty that I'm not helping out at this event, but I've already devoted a hundred hours or more to organizing the Women's Open. It was hard to not respond to the emails requesting volunteers on QChat. A banquet like this is a feat of coordination and weeks of planning, and requires teams to set up, serve, and clean. It's a huge stream of labour for the sake of one evening of feasting and pleasure. I sit down for a few moments with Team Pig and those keeping them company through their nightwatch. Steve reassures me by saying that everyone at this club has their role, and I've found mine. I yawn, looking forward to my bed. I can help out next year, bring a video camera, make a fun short film about the event. According to Richard Slee, the club's first pig roast was held in 1974, and I'm assured it'll happen again next year. I watch someone use a mop to baste the pig with sauce. I read the recipe on a table in the snug, but I have decided not to reveal it here.

Twenty hours later, a parrot is perched on the shoulder of a woman ahead of me in line. We all admire it and stroke its feathers. The lineup for the pig roast is so long that it snakes around the clubhouse. It's busier even than Lobsterfest. I sip a beer as I move slowly forward, chatting with my fellow diners. The smell of spicy meat and rich juices hangs over the lagoon. There's a live band and dancing on the lawn and a bouncy castle and kids sticking feathers to crowns at the arts-and-crafts table Beth and I set up. My plate is loaded with various cuts of pork, crackling, corn, and salads. Team Pig has excelled and the shreds of meat are so tender they barely require chewing. But I don't go for seconds. These feasts remind me of the Chinese family banquets where my sister and I learned to pace ourselves through ten courses by taking slow, small bites. Sometimes the rich variety of dishes—the cold blanched chicken, the steamed fish with ginger and scallion, the lobster with garlic and chilies, the red BBQ pork—stirred uneasily in my stomach. I preferred our quiet family dinners, without our watchful aunties, of my mom's stir-fries and clear soups, the steaming jasmine rice. Banquets are exciting, but it's simple cooking that nourishes me.

September nips at my heels as I walk sockless in boat shoes over the lawn.

Mark assigns me to the foredeck, Phil on jib trim, and Tala on the main, which will be her first time in the position. We're a bit shorthanded for the QCYC Open Regatta, but nearly everyone else is too. It's the Saturday in September after the pig roast, and there are big licks of wind south of Toronto Island. The racecourse is set up in the wedge of lake between the island's shoreline and the end of the Leslie Street Spit. There aren't enough boats registered for non-flying sails to split up the fleets into smaller PHRF ranges, so, unusually, *Panache* and the similarly rated *Dove* and *Hour Time* are racing against the bigger-sized *Circe III, Amelia, Roo,* and *Bandoleer.* Because of this, we finish in the back half of the fleet, and while this is a bit demoralizing, it's to be expected. "If we finish fourth overall, that's a very good effort," I say to the others, wanting to be realistic. What's more taxing is that we have less time between races than the bigger boats who finish faster. Still, we have a good rhythm, with Tala and Phil working hard on the upwind legs, and Mark passing the jib sheet to me to trim on downwind legs. After the third race, though, we're shaken at having to protest a boat in the flying sails fleet that called for room at the mark without an overlap, and that attempted to squeeze in anyway, causing us to veer off course.

"Should we do the fourth race?" Mark asks, somewhat unenthusiastically. Phil and I don't answer, but Tala is determined and fervent, putting the rest of us to shame. Mark, in a fit of what-do-we-have-to-lose, starts us on a port tack. Giving me a huge scare, *Amelia* suddenly appears, crossing within a few feet of our bow on starboard. I scramble up to the foredeck to look behind the jib, realizing that as the "give way" boat, we are threading through a gauntlet of yachts plowing full-speed ahead. We manage to avoid collision and escape unscathed.

Afterwards, we park ourselves at a picnic table on the lawn by the flagpole and are soon surrounded by the racers we have been competing against all day. Yuri of *Dove* wants my thoughts on how the racing rules apply to barging. Bruce joins us and asks me if I would mind talking the musician into playing a bit longer, and Josh dips his hand into my bag of chips before joining the Mazzas and Vanderwals seated behind us. Charles Waterman, president of Broad Reach Canada, is MCing the after-party, as he did last year, and he always infuses it with his Caribbean flavour. Every serving of rum punch has a stick of sugarcane in it, and I have at least three cups. Broad Reach is a non-profit that supports under-represented youth in sailing and funds sailing adventures for newcomers and marginalized kids and teenagers. It's another place I've been meaning to volunteer. But not now, I'm too hungry. My dinner ticket gets me a hot dog, a burger, and · salad, and I share my plate with Tala. The food is especially satisfying after the rigours of a regatta. Amazingly, *Panache* has won a third-place flag. We hadn't realized how much time other boats owed us. Mark lets Tala hold it for the evening, crediting her enthusiasm for our excellent overall finish. How simple it is to be happy—a coloured nylon triangle, a plate shared with someone else.

It becomes too much trouble to stay late at QCYC after a party and to return on an early-morning tender for a regatta so I ask Mark if I can sleep on *Panache*. In mid-September, I attend a viewing of the historical films from the 1930s to the 1980s about the club that Richard Slee is showing in the Great Hall, and stay overnight for an AHMEN race the next morning. Peter Jones, who joined the club in 1957, and Allen Rae Jr., who joined in 1958, are both in attendance, sitting at a table to the left of me. One of the clips shows an interview from 1987 between the two long-time friends about

their years racing International 14s. I know Al Rae as a fellow Pisces, a giver of great hugs, and the former skipper of
Enkidu, a Santana 525 that was a perennial Wednesday-night
winner. I know that Pat Whetung crewed with him, and, from
Wayne Lilley, that "in keeping with QCYC tradition, Al has
long mentored other racers, sharing skills acquired over sixty
years… Though no longer a boat owner, Al is still in demand
on Wednesday nights as guest crew or skipper. His prote-
ges, meanwhile, are sprinkled through QC's racing fleets and
remember Al's style at the helm." I wonder what it feels like
to be a member of a club for so long, and what flood of associations must come from walking through the club and seeing
its trees, building, and boats like a crowd of extended family.

"Some things never change," says a deep, sonorous voice at a
table beside me. We're watching a clip of members drinking
on their boats or by the lockers, playing without sound. The
images are grainy, jerky, and no one here was alive to remember exactly what was going on. Richard speaks about the difficulty in pinning down dates. He's committed to trying to figure
out when certain club traditions were inaugurated by speaking
to members and sifting through archives and documents, but
it's an elusive project. No one knew ahead of time that a post-
work party gathering might become a tradition, and when it
did, it was hard to recall how or who had started it. Many of
the club's traditions resist attempts to secure them in the past.

I slide the heavy, darkened plexiglass inserts and close *Panache*'s
hatchway from the inside. Across the lagoon, I hear cloudless

laughter, the whoosh of a beer can tab. I change into a T-shirt and cotton drawstring pants. The cabin is lit inside with small lights, the windows papered over with old magazines. The silence wraps around me and I hear the faint lick of water and the tinkling of metal shackles against shrouds. I feel soothed, sleeping on the water, in a way that I'm not on land. I go to bed earlier without internet and the lure of YouTube. I should always sleep on a boat or a houseboat. As I drift away I dream of the names of a vessel that I don't yet own, the address to a home I don't yet know.

Things I miss because I'm spending weekends on the island: fall book launches and festivals, a screening of a TIFF movie I have a ticket for, a second date with a Korean Canadian painter at Nuit Blanche, street food festivals, and the salmon run on the Humber River.

Things I've missed at the club because I have a life outside it: Friday-night trivia where a giant Stanley Cup–like trophy made of tinfoil was awarded, a dance party on the deck of the old *Rapids Queen*, yoga on Sunday mornings. I miss the awards banquet at the end of September because I have a craving to walk the trails of Odell Park in Fredericton and to immerse myself for two days of poetry readings at the university where I spent eight months as a writer-in-residence. I will always be missing something because of how quickly I'm filled to the brim.

When I wake up, the island is still and full of motion at the same time. I brush my teeth and spit into the water below, where dragonflies are skimming. The dew's already dry. I walk across the bridge to get a croissant and Americano at the Runaway Cafe kiosk. I write while waiting for the rest of the crew to show up for the Sunday AHMEN race, then roll up my sleeping bag. In the *Clipper*, board members have nicknamed last summer "the Summer of Endless Fun," and they occasionally referred to this year as "the Summer of Endless Fun, Part 2." The leaves are edged with yellow, fading from the outside in. Things are always ending—races, parties, summer evenings' long regress—but they are also always beginning. There's no escape from this continuous loop of the seasons, which I accept the way that I accept the tilted axis of the world.

Racing Log

Wednesday-night race—August 2, 2023

We had a full complement of crew for a Wednesday-night race in early August—Mark, Pat, Amanda, Tala, Phil, Quentin, and I. On jib trim were Phil (for his muscle) and Tala (to give her more practice), Pat was on main, and Amanda, Quentin, and I were ballast on foredeck. The weather radar had forecast 16 km of wind that morning, but I expected it to die down by the evening, and was hopeful there would be 4–5 knots for the race. Previous weeks had brought light wind, though it hadn't been as humid as summers past. Each week had seen an increase in wind, so it worked out well that our new associate members had more opportunities to feel how the boat handled at various degrees of speed.

There are a number of knowns and unknowns in writing. These do not remain static throughout a writer's practice. In the beginning, a writer might not even know themselves to be a writer. They may or may not know the discipline, sacrifices, disillusionments, and highs still to come. They may or may not know what makes for good writing, what makes for a narrative that races to the finish, what images can control language's waywardness. They may not know their own process—what times of day they're most focused, which rituals facilitate writing, whether to carefully outline their work or to free-write, how to adapt to the flow of where the writing takes them, how to rework a draft until it achieves the balance they are looking for.

With so many hands on board, I found myself on the bow for nearly the entirety of the evening. I had barely sat in the cockpit since my return from BC. I stood holding the mooring lines, waiting for the motor to start. Riley was on the boat beside us, Bandoleer, and I asked about his sangria recipe, hoping to enlist him to recreate it for the Women's Open party. I was so distracted that the crew had to alert me that Mark was ready to cast off. As we headed out of the lagoon, I could see the orange inflatable buoys set up in the northeast corner of the harbour for a triangle course. A new habit I'd adopted on the foredeck was to help the sails up, sliding them into the tracks, jiggling the reefing and cunningham lines, ready in case something got caught. I also used the opportunity to scope out the start line and to estimate which end had more wind and was closer to the upwind mark. I've always had difficulty trying to align the start line with the wind direction from the vantage point of the bow. The course resembled a skinny isosceles triangle on its side, with a longer upwind leg and two shorter reaching legs. It wasn't a large course and it felt as though we were squished into the corner of the harbour. At least we were out of the way of the ferry, though a city cruise boat drifting around Ward's Island appeared, as usual, totally undeterred by the 20–30 sailboats going at full speed.

There is a lot of advice about the craft of writing, especially for those starting out. Read widely, write every day, try out forms and techniques, put in the time, and so on. I have done all of these things, along with mumbling lines of my poems on walks to work out their rhythm, taking all the line breaks out and putting them back in, revising stories by switching a third-person perspective to the first. What I didn't know was how to form a habit or ritual of writing. My habits came from circumstances—walking along train tracks when I couldn't stand to be at my desk any longer, writing in notebooks on two-hour commutes, pulling out book proofs during my lunch breaks. Scoping out the long, cherry-lined streets, trudging across fields, the cityscape seeping into my skin and embodying itself in metaphors. Thinking about writing until those thoughts could not be contained was what made not writing feel nearly torturous. How does one cultivate the writing habit when trust in the necessity of writing hasn't come yet? It felt, for a long time, like I was going through the motions of making writing a muscle memory. What advice is there on how writing lives in the body?

A minute before our start, we were sailing on a beam reach and port tack, and near the pin end we had to duck below Fine Wine *on a starboard tack. Unexpectedly,* Spirit Warrior *crossed, and though we might've been able to make it without going down, Mark heeded our alarmed cries and we ducked them with a few feet to spare, crossing the start line and clearing the race committee boat and continuing on the port tack as the give-way boat. These manoeuvres kept Tala alert—she had to both ease the jib and then quickly sheet it in as tight as possible, because continuing for too long on a beam reach might result in a collision with the committee boat. Later, Mark said that he was a little late and had originally planned to also tack on starboard, but the mark boat was in the way. Which was strange— usually they would've motored away from the pin to keep the line clear. Ultimately, going over to the right side of the course worked out in our favour.*

To start a piece of writing is to give way to an impulse, like the urge to trail your hand into a fountain or to turn your face into the sun. In the moment, the why may not be evident— the impulse only begins to feel more and more unbearable the longer it is put off. Sometimes the reasons for delay are fear, lack of clarity, or lack of trust in the thing that needs to be written down. If I attempt to dismiss the otherworldly flashes and images that appeared to me, they would come less and less frequently, until a kind of starvation sets in and the body forgets it has need to sustain imagination. To begin a piece of writing is not the same as finding its beginning. That can come later. When I was younger, I had to be pushed to start. These days, I make ready, clenching my hands, waiting to receive.

I kept waiting to observe the boats in our fleet tacking over and either going below or above us, unable to see behind Panache's opaque genoa. But as we tacked beyond the layline and neared the mark, no one was even close, much to my satisfaction. Tala was a little slower than Phil in sheeting in the jib until it was nearly touching the spreaders, and I reminded myself to pass on my own tricks to getting the sail over before it filled out and the pressure on the sail made it so much more difficult to sheet in. We had clear air leaving the mark to port and going on a broad reach toward the next mark, near the wall at Polson and Cherry Streets, and then gybing on another reach to the rounding mark near the race committee boat.

You write the first draft for yourself and later drafts for your readers. This does not mean a relinquishing of intention or vision, but a reorientation, like seeing the work from another point in time and space. It can be difficult to reorient to the reader's position, coming from the inside of the mechanics of image and narrative that, for the writer, creak and chug along. Each component—word choice, phrase, sentence, page of dialogue, exposition, or action—can feel discrete and oily for the writer. The nuts and bolts of writing. But when the work is newly forged, it is necessary to take oneself out of it. To make a small crevice for the reader to occupy. A writer is someone who builds a house they never plan to live in themselves.

The five-minute starting sequences for each fleet serve to separate out the faster boats from the slower, and also to stagger them around the course. We were often on a downwind or reaching leg when the next fleet started, but this wasn't always the case. Our first lap had gained us such an advantage, so Mark followed nearly the same route up the course for our next lap. As we headed back upwind, I observed the fastest PHRF 1 fleet, including Blue Streak, Circe III, Amelia, *and* Veloce, *crossing the start line. I sighed inwardly, anticipating that these larger keelboats would barrel over us, negating the advantage we had gained over* On the Rocks *and* Fine Wine, *who we owed time. The fleet split into starboard and port tacks, some perhaps following our course after watching where we'd found wind in the centre of the harbour. Since I wasn't required to set the whisker pole, I occupied myself with calling the gusts so Pat could ease the main before they caused the boat to round up. Gusts appeared on the water as slightly darker patches or stripes, but their angle of movement could be tricky to determine. Another way to find gusts is to watch the boats ahead to see if they suddenly heel and round into the wind. I also watched the PHRF 1 boats start to pile up behind each other, with the exception of* Blue Streak, *which had gained nearly a leg on its competitors.*

I cannot tell when and if I have written well. I only know that if the work has a quality of soundness, like a bell, and if I no longer have the desire to climb back into it and rewrite it, then it has integrity for me. When I reread my past work that has this cooled, forged quality, I worry that I will never be able to write as well again. It's true that I am in a different place and time, and therefore the way toward and into the work will always happen from a different position. But I have always felt a sense of disconnect from the things I make—a knitted scarf, a line drawing, a meal. It is as though the work disowns me once I'm no longer immersed in the process of making it. Completing a manuscript brings on a period of mourning, because what I love best is to be inside a project, even as I rush toward its completion the way lovers rush toward their release.

By the next lap, Circe *and* Veloce *had nearly reached the windward mark and taken each other up on the first reaching leg, with* Amelia *close behind. As* Panache *reached toward the gybe mark, we were able to get an overlap and to nimbly round the mark on the inside. As we eased out the sails on the reaching leg, I fully expected all three boats to overtake us. Crouching on the low side of the boat,*

I pretended not to be concerned. The rest of the crew had on their best game faces as well. I liked to think it was out of goodwill toward Mark that Circe *and* Veloce *didn't come down on us, but he also took care to steer up a few times to assert our position.*

There is no use comparing yourself to other writers. It's difficult not to do so, though, when the novels and plays and short stories and poetry of other writers are also models. More than that, they are beacons through the unrelenting conditions of life. But at some point, a writer has to chart their own course. I have come to realize that I don't have another writer's ferocity of vision, or instinct for formal innovation, but I have my own kind of toughness. My own assertions about the frayed land, or the ties of time, or the cyclical nature of fallacy, that I fiercely maintain.

I squinted at skipper Ron Mazza on Circe *and Chris, who was helming his dad's boat,* Amelia. *On shore both would usually wave and grin at me, but in their cockpits they looked determined and deep in concentration. I turned my attention to what I was supposed to be doing, communicating the tickler play back to Tala and estimating the number of boat lengths to the next mark. I was glad when the race committee boat sounded our finish and* Panache *was relieved of the collective pressure from the big boats. Boats have a body language, and it's possible to feel frustration, confusion, hesitation, or triumph emanating from them like a vapour.* Panache's *plucky spirit always put us in these dramatic situations, which I only laughed at once we were safely finished with the race. I was already anticipating recapping and retelling our race, making it into an account that could be given away, housed in another form.*

Lifelines

Saturday, May 7, 2022

I've managed everything on my own somehow—packing and shipping my books from Fredericton, flying back to Toronto on a Monday night with three suitcases, moving into my new apartment, unpacking, and setting up the creative writing course I'll be teaching online next week. There's no rest for the wicked, except I don't even have time to be wicked. I'll add it to my to-do list, after writing a syllabus and setting up my internet.

I took a video of my apartment to send Dad, to reassure him that it's safe and comfortable and has bars on the windows—though I felt like I'd made a mistake when I saw it in person for the first time. The floor is laminate wood, the bathroom fixtures are flimsy and old, and it's smaller than it looked in the photos. But in the morning, light douses the white walls, the ceilings are high, and there's a gas stove, lots of countertops, and a front porch for people-watching.

Dad keeps sending me condo listings, but the idea of living in a glass box in the sky is about as appealing as being shrink-wrapped. I know his insistence on my building equity comes from love mixed with worry. When I next visit BC, I'll try to explain to him that there are too many what-ifs keeping me from buying my own place. Do I even want to live in Toronto, for instance? Part of me wishes I had stayed in New Brunswick, where a house doesn't cost the royalties of the TV series I haven't written or sold. I miss the trails papered with leaves and quiet. I miss how everyone's house is a ten-minute walk away. I even miss the slick uphill hike to my office on campus. I have to remind myself why I returned—my job, my publisher, my community, sailing.

I'd been so looking forward to sailing again, but *Panache* is currently under repairs. It'll be weeks before the boat's hull is fixed. In the meantime, Pat recommended that Amanda and I attend the participants' meeting at the club next week—lots of skippers will be there. The thought of crewing on someone else's boat makes me nervous, but that's a sign I should do it.

I went on a date last night. More on that later. Sleep first!

Friday, May 20, 2022
With half my week in the learning centre and the other half teaching, I feel flattened, like the empty cardboard boxes I've taken out to the recycling bin. When I need a break from my to-do lists, I unpack and hang pictures and replace the grody old bathroom cabinet with my big square mirror, which gives me energy. I've ordered a rolling rack made by a local furniture maker and found a yoga studio just a five-minute walk away.

A few weeks ago, I was hanging out in the first neighbourhood I lived in, near Ossington and Bloor. My date arrived frazzled and late after trying to find parking. Tall, lean, fit, blondish, and slightly grumpy, Wesley's a former chef and single dad. A Virgo with a Scorpio rising, "I should hate everything," he joked. We got along well enough that after drinks at Northwood we jaywalked across Bloor for dinner at Banjara, talking about astrology, food, and foraging. We've hung out a few times since. I enjoy his company, but it bothers me that he comes to my house empty-handed. Clearly, we were brought up with different values. He's also a secretive, closed-off man. While he always responds when I text, he rarely invites or instigates. I saw his capacity for kindness when he told me about surprising his daughter after school with a trip to the wave pool, but I don't want to continue a casual relationship for months and months in the hopes that I'll eventually be a recipient of his generosity. Maybe I should be less picky, but I have self-respect.

Friday, May 27, 2022
Finally got out on a boat this week, thanks to Eric Whan of *Alpha Omega* kindly inviting Amanda and me after the participants' meeting. I was embarrassed when Pat announced to the whole room that we were looking for a boat to crew on, but it had the intended effect. I've known Eric for a while—he used to come over to hang out at the Badlands from time to time, and now that I think about it, he's one of the earliest skippers at the club who remembered my name and took the time to get to know me.

I've never raced on any boat other than *Panache* so I didn't know what to expect. I even got a little lost trying to find *Alpha* because it's docked on the other side of the lagoon. It's a J/30, a bigger boat than *Panache*, and it races in the PHRF 1 or 2 fleets. The deck is also steeper, and Eric warned us that it could be slippy, which I appreciated. I joined his daughter, Olive, and his partner, Anna-Christina, who showed me the boat set-up. I noted small differences, like how they roll their main instead of flaking it, where they store their whisker pole, etc., but the essentials are the same. Follow directions, get the pole up, trim the jib. The biggest difference is crewing with a family, though when I think about it, maybe every crew has ongoing discussions and tensions and love that extend beyond what takes place during a race. They have that shared history.

Monday, May 30, 2022

Continuing my adventures boat-hopping, I crewed on *Circe III* last weekend for the ABYC regatta. I'm a little intimidated by Ron Mazza—he has a reputation for running a tight ship. But when he emailed me the details of the race, I knew I shouldn't miss out on the experience. It's one of the fastest boats at the club. I just managed to squeeze onto the 9:15 a.m. pontoon boat that for some weird reason the club sent over instead of the *Algonquin Queen II,* and then one of our crew got left behind and we had to wait for him. So Ron was under a bit of a cloud when we motored late from the dock. We were also late for the first race but still managed to catch up to the rest of the fleet.

Foredeck is a three-person job on *Circe.* I've never seen anything like their level of coordination. Sue and Nansi, two sisters who have crewed with Ron for decades, took such good care of me, showing me the layout of the boat and the exact spot to sit to avoid being caught in the jib sheets when the boat tacked. I volunteered to hook the pole to the jib and I think they appreciated my willingness. So that's basically all I did for four races, hook and unhook the pole, because it had to be threaded through the shrouds in a very specific order. I can't believe how tired I got just trying to get the pole up and down as fast as possible. I prefer the rotating style of *Panache*, but doing the same thing over and over again certainly reduces confusion. Sue and Nansi were very impressed when I skirted the jib by myself—not sure why.

Circe is a Viking 34 so it handles big wind very differently from what I've been used to. We did quite well, winning the next two races and coming in second overall. It was so interesting to watch Ron constantly make adjustments. I know he used to be a Shark sailor when he first joined the club. He keeps a blog too—I wonder if he's ever thought of writing a book. I should ask him. I don't feel scared of him anymore.

Speaking of books, I finally caved to Andrew's gentle pressure and wrote a sailing essay. It seemed to just roll out of me. So I think I'll write another. I feel energized by teaching this creative writing class, even though it's a grind. Every week I write lectures, make presentations, record and upload them, grade assignments, and then do it all over again. The students' work is strong and fresh when they can be convinced to give up their idea of what they think good writing is.

Thursday, June 23, 2022
I found out from Mom that Dad asks her constantly for updates about me. Why doesn't he email, or call, or text me? It's confounding. She also let me know that he's been selling his work online on Saatchi Art and the site recently featured two of his paintings. I've given up nagging him to have his work professionally photographed, to put together a portfolio, to submit to gallery open calls. I know he's ambitious, but I can't understand his paranoia that someone might steal his

work, or his reluctance to self-promote. I should email Mom more, even as busy as I am.

I have just one more class to teach and final portfolios to grade, and then this crazy schedule will be over. As a break, I'm off to Saskatchewan with Amanda to visit Joanne and her family for the long weekend, finally reuniting the three of us for the first time since Joanne joined the faculty at U of Saskatoon. And then I can finally properly enjoy the summer, though at least sailing has provided a break from being chained to my desk. My last dinghy class is tomorrow, and I've crewed twice more on *Alpha*. The weather's been all over the place this month, sweltering and windless one week, and super-gusty another week. Eric's always calm and thinking a few steps ahead, so he won't ask us to hoist the sails until he's sure the race won't be cancelled. On the week it was Eric's turn to be race officer, he asked Rachel from *L'Otago* to sub in for him as skipper, to give her an opportunity to helm more. We came in second one week. Eric's daughter, Olive, can get the jib in all on her own, and after watching her I figured out how to use the fancy self-tailing jib winch. Eric even told me I was a fast learner. We might even have come in first if I'd been a little faster. Again with the self-criticism! It's such a hard habit to break.

Tuesday, July 5, 2022

Back home after a shimmering long weekend spent walking the stretched streets of Saskatoon with Giul and Jo's two retrievers, brunches, a peony farm, gin cocktails, eating idlis with Amanda's aunt, medicine plant walks at Wanuskewin, and many, many good meals under the canopy of summer. I miss them already, and need more days like those.

I have my first session with a psychotherapist next week. After all, I have health benefits and I've gone through the list like a menu, trying naturopathy, osteopathy, massage. It's clear I need a better work/life balance, better boundaries, all those things that have sprung into the modern lingo of self-care but that I still can't quite enact. There must be a better way than being trapped in the revolving turnstile of my mind, of agreeing to do too much, feeling resentful, getting burned out, not being able to do any work, and feeling needlessly guilty for resting. I have an email inbox full of manuscripts to read for Brick Books' editorial board next month, and a meeting with my new mentee next week. It never ends, but also, this is what I signed up for.

Saturday, July 9, 2022
My new industrial pipe and walnut wood bookcase arrived last week. The designer, Brittany, delivered it herself. I couldn't do anything except arrange books for a few days.

The bookcase, the rolling rack, and the new houseplants are counterbalancing my exasperation with this apartment, with its insects and fetid water smell seeping through the vents. I wonder if I could replace the showerhead myself. My landlord is quite fond of me because of how clean I am, but still, I don't want to ask him to do anything I can't do myself.

Other than house projects, I feel like I've hardly gotten anything done lately. It's summer, though. And *Panache* is repaired and good as new. Finally, Mark, Pat, Tim, Phil, Amanda, and I are racing together again. We cannot thank Paul enough for his help with the repairs. Also, Mark heard glowing feedback about Amanda and me from the other skippers. I think it's important to leave a good impression, being a guest on someone else's boat. It's comforting to return to muscle memory and familiarity with my crew, but also good to remember that I have options.

Friday, July 29, 2022

One of the first things my therapist asked me to do was to make a list of every commitment and project on my plate right now, everything taking up time and energy. And when I did it, there were over forty items! Not all of them were active, such as my short story collection, on pause until I can figure out how to write fiction—an important step. My third poetry collection will need a couple more years of steeping and trickling. I'm proliferating unfinished manuscripts. Now it's looking like I may be writing a collection of sailing essays. I have that feeling of disappearing into sentences when I'm writing it, something I haven't felt for I don't know how long.

I'm off to Ottawa to spend a few days there, then up to Sault Ste. Marie. Dad texted to see if I would come to BC for a rest after teaching and I felt so guilty that I needed time alone for writing instead. This guilt that I'm feeling is a projection—I know my parents will understand.

Monday, October 10, 2022

I regret not racing the Last Chance Cup a few weeks ago before the awards banquet, because now it looks like my last race was a really gusty AHMEN race we had to abandon because Mark's cousin felt sick. Not that I blame him—the waves were so high that I couldn't see the pin end of the starting line. Mark put me on mainsail trim for the first time, since I had more experience than the others. I kept having to dump the main when I felt *Panache* heeling too much and then sheeting it in again. "Is this what Pat and Amanda do?" I asked Mark. He seemed surprised at my question, which shows that if he's not having to correct me, I must be doing it right.

Now that sailing season is over, I should make an effort to date more again. What with working, writing, sailing, and socializing, it's hard to find the time. I wonder if that's an excuse, though, because in my past dating experience, my boyfriends have sapped my energy and exhausted me emotionally. I refuse to believe in this pessimistic mantra of there being no good men left. I think my singleness has more to do with constantly not prioritizing my own health and happiness. It sends a message to other people that my needs don't matter.

Fall To-Do List:
   Book a writing retreat over Labour Day weekend (Haliburton? Picton?)
   Finish and submit sailing book proposal
   Continue with book research and drafting
   Prioritize health (sailing, swimming, yoga, walks, psychotherapy)
   Try to maintain a regular sleep schedule
   Check in regularly with my body; it knows best

Tuesday, December 13, 2022
Nearly missed my flight, thanks to the long security lineup at Pearson, but I made it to my parents' apartment in glassy Richmond. I wanted an extra week with them, but working on Pacific time has posed some logistical challenges, like trying not to wake my dad when I'm delivering workshops on Teams at 7:00 a.m. Mom's spoiled me with steamed crab and lunch every day. It's amazing the enormous amount of time I

save when I don't have to cook. Dad tells me what new pieces he's working on but mostly stays inside to watch the news or stacks of documentaries, sometimes talking at me for hours and sometimes barely looking up.

When I look at Dad, I see so many qualities we share. His sensitivity, introversion, the hours he spends quietly resting after waking, his digestive issues, and eczema are all in me, but more diluted, more manageable. I see the effects of our different parenting—Dad's likely on the autism spectrum: it runs on that side of the family. Because of Nai-Nai and Aunt Alice's mocking, he takes rejections and setbacks much more to heart than I do. He tells me about not getting responses to submissions, not meeting deadlines, his expression discouraged. I urge him to apply for everything, but I understand now that this is much more difficult for him than it is for me. I have parents who believe that there's nothing out of my reach. I can apply to things and forget about them, and most of the time I forget the rejections too. I wonder what could've been if Dad had received the love and belief he gave his daughters—and I feel such a sense of loss.

Sunday, February 12, 2023
Something broke in me during the pandemic and I feel like I'm holding myself up to the light, trying to find the fracture so I can repair it. Like that Japanese art of filling in the seams of broken pottery with glue and powdered gold.

I turn forty-two in a few weeks. Went for drinks with a thirty-eight-year-old jazz bass player who asked me if I liked younger men. "I don't," I said, though I told him that I had a good feeling about him. We have the same sense of humour, and I like how his face crumples when he laughs. He was so curious about my books, the collection of objects I have around my apartment, but I think I've misjudged him. In fact, I know I have. "It's an act," he said as he was leaving, when I commented on how sweet he seemed. Maybe I'm a bad judge of character when it comes to men, though eventually I catch on. I'm starting to distrust my own ability to choose the right partner.

Thursday, April 6, 2023
Amanda had her birthday party at the club last weekend. It was so much fun to BBQ there and hang out in the snug. I baked a chai-flavoured cake and brought it over on the ferry to feed the dozens of sailors from St. James Town and QCYC. Everyone's excited about launch in a couple of weeks, as am I.

I had an essay, "Boat Words," accepted by *Brick* magazine for their upcoming issue on the theme of water. I'm taking a month-long leave of absence in June to go to Kingston, visit my parents, and write as much as I possibly can. Hopefully it will push me out of my procrastination this past winter and spring. I feel stalled with writing, and instead of sleeping I endlessly doomscroll, read feel-good romance novels, and indulge in other forms of escapism. But, thanks to the work with my psychotherapist, who recommended Tricia Hersey's *Rest Is Resistance*, I also feel less guilty about resting every day, about leaving a party early, and opting out of attending book launches and literary events. Especially when I think about that giant list of commitments. I don't have the time or energy to add more to my day. This is progress.

Thursday, June 14, 2023
I'm well into my month of absence and managed to finish a

long essay on club history and community while in Kingston. I've never visited the city before. It's reminiscent of Ottawa, with its limestone buildings, brick mansions, and yards full of daylilies and poppies. I spooked myself by taking a ghost trolley tour and then imagining unhappy Victorians peeking out at me as I walked back to my Airbnb. I sailed on a big J35 out of Kingston Yacht Club. They have a great "no body left behind" policy, and anyone who contacts the membership chair can crew on one of the PHRF 1 fleet boats. Even with seven of us, we were still short-handed, with just myself and a sailing instructor in his twenties on the bow. I felt stressed with all the lines and shackles, especially because they fly a spinnaker on their weeknight races, which I haven't done all season. When it came time to douse it, I wasn't able to release the end of the spinnaker pole—I couldn't figure out or see the mechanism because it was stuck behind the jib, and the skipper had to come up to get it done and yelled at me to get back to the cockpit. I didn't listen to her, though—I couldn't abandon my crewmate on the bow. I did redeem myself by getting a halyard untangled from the open hatch and managing the rest of the race without mishaps. It occurs to me now that I've never been yelled at before on a race, not by Mark, Eric, Ron, or any other male skipper.

It was still a beautiful sail on the lake, with the windmills on Wolfe Island in the distance, and I learned some new tactics. We had a debrief after and I apologized for not getting myself familiar with all the shackles beforehand—each one was different. We still came in fourth overall. I think the skipper forgave me, because she invited me to come back any time. But I wonder if I'm really suited to race on anything bigger than thirty feet.

Thursday, June 22, 2023

Flew to BC on the 18th, which I forgot was Father's Day and my parents' wedding anniversary. We had lobster and Prosecco, but Dad dislikes gifts, always says I should save my hard-earned money. When we were younger, we used to make him birthday cards and bake cakes, but he said they only made him remember the birthdays he'd had without them. Most of Dad's aversions are based on things that remind him of his mother—Shanghainese food, knitting needles, I forget what else. It's hard to keep track.

My mom and I are now in Victoria for five days to give her a much-needed break from cooking, cleaning, and Dad's particularities. I invited Dad but he refused, saying he would welcome the time on his own. Still, I hope he isn't feeling too lonely. Mom shows me the funny texts he sends her before bedtime. I feel bad for being frustrated with him and unloading on her. Dad didn't go for anger management counselling until I was away at university, and she says all the time that she wishes she'd urged him to seek help much sooner. I tell her it's not her fault, that it's common for a lot of immigrant families to not know these supports exist. He hasn't lost his temper since, though he sometimes still gets moody. I have to acknowledge how much he's healed. But although the wounds aren't raw and open anymore, I can still feel tender spots, spots I don't press on too hard.

Sunday, July 16, 2023

We have some new faces on *Panache*! Tim moved to Europe and I was away in Vancouver, so Mark found Jade and Tala on the crew bank. They're new associate members, without any previous experience, but very smart and eager to learn. They seem to already have friends at the club and they're always bringing snacks and drinks. After one race, Jade tried her hand at helming while Pat directed us all to sit on the high and low sides so she could feel the difference with steering. Tala followed me around the foredeck and wanted to know how to hook up the jib, tie bowlines, etc. They've both also volunteered to help with the Women's Open Regatta.

I suppose I shouldn't find it strange that I'm starting to have a lot of opinions about sailing, with all this writing, research, racing, and volunteering. After all, I'm so opinionated about everything else. What has felt outside myself is to be talking with Bruce or Paul or Mark or Steve Hill and hear judgments and boat-speak unexpectedly come out of my mouth. Even if I'm wrong, I think it's better to express opinions and to ask questions because I learn more that way. I'm still quite con-flict-averse, and have difficulty breathing and thinking when I hear raised voices. Fortunately, I've never heard of violent shouting matches happening at the club. Mark has told me that even when he's volunteered at protest hearings, skippers remain calm, reasonable, and congenial toward each other. I don't think I could be a member otherwise.

Thursday, August 24, 2023
Mark's away in New Brunswick so nearly the entire crew of *Panache* lent themselves out to Neale Martin, owner and skip-per of *Meridian*. It was his first race! It was so weird to be the most experienced crew member aboard, and I wasn't force-ful enough about telling Neale to head closer to the start line when we motored out—I think he was nervous about colli-sions. There was maybe a knot of wind, so we kept stalling

when trying to tack toward the start, even with Jade, Tala, Phil, and a friend of Neale's all perched on the low side. Neale took it all with good humour, though, and was able to laugh about it afterwards, telling everyone that the race committee removed the starting pin before we could make it over the line! He bought us jugs of beer and the crew of *Caetera* joined us. They'd done much better and won their fleet. I was happy for *Caetera*'s skipper, Josh—I think it's only his second time racing his boat.

Jade and Tala have also been crewing with Paul and Jeremy Horne on *Kiku*, a J/22, and it looks like I too will be a gun for hire for the next few weeks.

Friday, September 1, 2023
I got a last-minute invite to crew on *Amelia* this week—Josh texted Tala, who texted me. I was so excited I forgot my self-imposed rule about not racing on big, scary boats. I've been curious about the Vanderwals for a long time because they used to own a Niagara 26. I don't know why I never introduced myself to Roel and his son Chris, who's about my age. QCYC social bubbles, I guess. But Josh spoke so warmly of them and says he's learned a lot. *Amelia*'s a Viking 33, like *Circe*, but has a completely different feel. It's quite spartan. They were short-handed and Chris put me on jib trim, which was a workout because it was quite a breezy night. "You need to turn the winch clockwise," Chris told me. "I am!" I huffed. It was embarrassing, but instead of getting frustrated he just started laughing, which made me laugh, which further delayed matters.

Amelia's crew are extremely polite and good at communication. I am constantly thanked. I think they have a hidden agenda because it makes me want to work harder. I found out they BBQ dinner for the crew after every race, and it's nice to be appreciated and fed. There's a lot to do on the boat, but it's certainly not boring. Still, I'm not sure I'm the best fit in terms of my strength and agility.

I can't believe it's Labour Day weekend already. It's a club-heavy weekend with a corn roast and a pig roast. It's been a good summer, maybe one of my happiest for a long time. I've spent so much time outdoors and on the water, and I don't feel guilty about it one bit.

Sunday, September 10, 2023

I'm starting to feel less like a writer who sails and more like a sailor who writes. The writer in me wants to use everything, share all of the jokes and quirks and stories and private lives of the sailing community, but the sailor in me knows that if I do that, no one would ever trust me again. There's lots I can't share in my book, personal stuff about health and addiction, complaints about the club and its programs, mistakes and fouls on the racecourse—everything you might expect in a tight-knit community full of relations and old friends and politics. I don't think it serves the community or the book to disclose the uncomfortable parts. Most of it is passing gossip that dissipates, and writing it down would give it more per-manence than it warrants. Some of the good yarns are meant to be told in person anyway and lose a lot of flavour on the printed page. I won't be able to fully capture the humour, the idiosyncrasies, the atmosphere, and the dramas that charac-terize the club on the page. There are some stories that aren't mine to share. After all, I want to be invited back.

Friday, September 22, 2023

Dad's birthday yesterday and Mom's tomorrow, so I usually call them on the day in between. Two Virgos, but they exhibit very different traits of the sign. Mom's the perfectionist, the one who can be very warm but also shy about new people, hates it when people are late, rude, or thoughtless. Dad can be particular, critical, and anxious, but at heart he's a healer, and when I visit he checks my blood pressure, shows me acupressure points, and tries to persuade me to see a Chinese herbal medicine doctor. For a time, he read my palm and analyzed my handwriting too.

I feel I ought to acquiesce because it's his way of showing care, but I feel pressured, which I know is very ungrateful of me. I'm impatient with having to accept his particular way of caretaking, but I try not to show it. I don't know why I have so much difficulty receiving care from men especially. It even feels uncomfortable not to cook or contribute to *Amelia*'s post-race dinners—I brought fruit and chocolate one night, because I wasn't raised to show up empty-handed.

Even though Mark is back, I've still been crewing with *Amelia* because *Panache* has plenty of bodies. I feel disloyal, but I wonder if I outgrew *Panache* years ago and didn't want to admit it. There's more discussion on *Amelia* about tactics, and even though I can't contribute much at this point, listening in on the eternal debate about To Tack Or Not To Tack is fascinating. We had enough crew a few weeks ago for me to be in my happy place on the bow, and we won the race on corrected time, and the jug of beer too. I told Mark about it and he thinks that now they'll never let me go. The last race of the season was last night, but, anticlimatically, there was almost no wind. Josh kept apologizing, as if it was his fault. Roel was stoic and silent as usual, while Chris yelped, "Pinching!" like he was physically pained by the luffing jib. Jeremy groused about motorboats driving through the course and then apologized for grousing, and Harrison, new to the club this season, looked like he was napping on the bow but was still useful as ballast. What a quirky bunch. I don't seem to have much in common with the guys on *Amelia,* but the more I get to know them, the more I realize I've found a fellow crew of introverts. No one yells, no one argues. I exhorted them to move out of the cockpit and onto the boat's leeward side to help induce heel, which I like to think helped somewhat. *Amelia* will pick up a second-place flag for the series.

We went up to the club to celebrate Bruce's birthday, and everyone came to show respect to the rear commodore, so I ended up drinking first with the *Amelia* crew and then with the *Panache* crew. Tala needs to stop ordering tequilas she can't or doesn't want to drink because she passes them to me. I am past the age of doing shots on a weekday night. My life is so difficult, isn't it?

Sunday, September 24, 2023

My last full weekend of racing. I'm bruised all over after the Donald D. Summerville Memorial Race at ABYC on Saturday and an AHMEN race on Sunday. It was just Roel, Ajay, and I on Saturday for the long-distance race, though it wasn't that long, only about six nautical miles. I felt nauseous because I didn't get enough sleep. I had met Ajay once before. He takes excellent photos, and I'd emailed him about using one for an author photo. He's from the UK, only moved to Toronto a few years ago. I think we only had to do five tacks the entire upwind leg because we were lifted so much. The Viking sure does well in big winds. Roel looked like he could've reached the water with one hand, *Amelia* was heeling so much. Somehow, with Ajay being so strong and efficient with hauling in the jib, the two of us managed all the trimming. Roel gives very little direction. He told me there was a time when *Amelia*'s crew all knew their jobs so well that no one needed to say much. This seems ideal to me.

There was a stretch, with the boat being lifted toward the upwind mark, with Ajay and me trying to be as much ballast as possible, and with none of the other boats in our fleet in sight, that I wanted to go forever. The day was gorgeous, just warm enough, and the lake looked so kind and happy to lift us on its back. We had one of the lifelines behind our backs so we could lean out as much as possible, with only that narrow cord keeping us from tumbling off the boat. I was almost disappointed when Ajay spotted the weather buoy. I never experienced anything like it on *Panache* because a smaller keelboat handles wind like that so differently. That sense of rush and speed could become addictive.

Roel had me take the wheel going home. I tended to veer too far in one direction, then overcorrect in the other direction. Next time, I'll try not to overthink it. I just checked the results online and *Amelia* did, in fact, win our fleet. Still hard to believe that we pulled it off short-handed and with a twenty-year-old sail. I won't forget this race quickly. I'll update on how the AHMEN race went tomorrow. I feel like my bed is rocking underneath me, rolling back and forth. I can't remember what's on my to-do list, but it doesn't matter. When I had trouble sleeping, Dad told me to tell myself I can always do what I need to tomorrow. I should follow his advice.

Many Hands

❑ The summer days are rich and brilliant, and you don't want to think about haulout. Except you have to start thinking about haulout because your yard chair has emailed a reminder to keep your boat cradles clear for inspection. Remove ladders, tarps, fenders, and dollies by the weekend. He apologizes for the short notice.

❑ It is mandatory for all senior members to attend both haulout weekends in October. Circle them in red in your calendar. Members who are unable to attend must make arrangements with other members to prepare their boat, unstep the mast, and secure the boat in the cradle after haulout.

❑ Check the cradle inspection report to ensure your boat's cradle is in good condition, and repair any rotten planks, cross members, uprights, etc.

❑ Remember to place your lumber order by the deadline.

❑ If you lack carpentry skills to build or repair a cradle, ask or bribe another member for help. Members who complain that no one is coming to their aid should remember that the best way to find help is to first offer it to others.

Rum, beer, and cigars are acceptable gifts in exchange for help, so stock up when they're on sale.

❑ Many hands make light work! Volunteers are required to off-load lumber delivery for yard prep and for installing temporary mast racks.

❑ Volunteers are required to remove the old woodblocks from the rail car, to clean and paint the car, and to install new blocks. Your yard chair will provide materials and tools. You can be proud that you have contributed to the upkeep and maintenance of a unique marine railway system that has been used since 1922!

❑ Choose a burnished fall day for one last sail. Afterwards, you may choose to shrink-wrap your memories under a waterproof and puncture-proof cover. This will protect them better from the harsh winter elements and insects than a tarp. However, shrink wrap cannot be removed and put back on, and you won't have access to your nostalgia until the spring.

❑ Consider a custom-made canvas or a polyester UV-resistant cover for your boat, which is more economical and environmentally friendly. Protect your investment!

❑ Empty out any water, fuel, and holding tanks on your boat so there is no danger of freezing over the winter or unpleasantness in the spring.

❑ Remove food, blankets, towels, clothing, and anything else that could make an attractive winter nest for mice and raccoons.

❑ Ensure that your mast is unstepped before haulout. Ensure that you use a strong line, not an old and frayed one. Wait until after your mast is unstepped to start drinking.

❑ If you are not prepared to do this amount of volunteer

labour, this club, with its self-help ethic, may not be for you. Perhaps a full-service club with its commensurate membership fees would be a better fit.

❑ Check in with members you know have health issues or are going through a difficult time, in case they are too proud to ask for assistance.

❑ In preparation for haulout, volunteers are needed to clear the dry sail area and install temporary ways. Your help is much appreciated!

❑ Wear appropriate work clothing in the yard at all times during haulout. Safety boots, gloves, and protective eyewear are highly recommended. Navy or tan cotton twill work coveralls will last many seasons and are universally flattering.

❑ Members are required to bring post-haulout beer from the city over on the *Algonquin Queen* and will be rewarded with many cheers.

❑ If anyone is in touch with _____, owner of _____, please reach out to the office, yard, and moorings. It is in regards to his plans for winter storage. We have not been able to make contact, and time is running out.

❑ Sailing is not only photo-worthy sunset cruises and thrilling races, but also greasy, tedious cleaning and maintenance jobs. In this hemisphere, your boat spends more time on the hard than in water. Sailing is also waiting. It is long winter sleeps. It is planning to buy or sell a boat. It is preparation.

❑ Members are required to like each other's winter activity Instagram posts. Members are required to respond to messages. Members are required.

You Don't Miss Much

AT FIRST GLANCE, YOU can't tell who the sailors are. They're not, as lore would have it, always smoking a pipe or wearing a navy blazer with club insignia and badges. But in a crowd, you might be able to deduce those who spend a great deal of time on the water through a process of elimination. It's probably not that woman in a fringed jacket and dangly earrings, or that hip-looking dude in tight, raw denim. It's more likely the dad in a saggy hoodie or that older woman in a Columbia rain jacket. It could be anyone in leggings, Henleys, or polarized sunglasses. It's that cyclist with the pannier bags loaded with beer, snacks, and rain gear, or the shopper moving efficiently through the aisles, grabbing frozen burger patties. Sperrys or boat shoes can be a giveaway, especially if the shoes look like they've seen better days, like if the leather sides are no longer stiff and the wearer is without socks. A red Mount Gay Rum cap or any other kind of baseball cap is also a signal, especially if you can spy collar clips, chinstraps, or sunglasses ties around their neck. They're wearing little to no makeup, and they're in need of a haircut, a shave, or both.

At some point, you're not sure when, you stopped buying uncomfortable shoes and considered every clothing purchase with water sports in mind. It became too much hassle to change in and out of work dresses and blouses, and since your workplace doesn't require formal office wear, you can show up in sturdy black jeans with a T-shirt under your button-up. You don't want anything restrictive, and you have a special love of pockets. You're constantly searching for comfortable pants with elastic waistbands, and when you find them, you buy three pairs. You have less patience for shopping anyway, as you're either saving for a boat or spending all your savings on boat maintenance, or both. You've realized that shopping is a balm for those who can't get out on the water—their unconscious misery assuaged by consumerism. You amass a collection of club and regatta shirts, beer glasses, and $20 sunglasses. Your closet now houses foul-weather gear, PFDs, coveralls, and workboots. You have regular sailing clothes, more or less your everyday wardrobe, and your fancy clothes for Sailpast and awards banquets—which means untorn jeans, white pants, striped Breton shirts from Armor-Lux or Old Navy, and yes, the obligatory navy blazer. When you go shopping, it's for a very specific brand of anti-fouling paint, marine sealant, snap shackles, a new VHS handheld radio, or portable food that can stay dry for weeks at a time. Your partner, kids, and family never have trouble buying you gifts—you appreciate plastic wineglasses, GPS trackers, wool socks and sweaters, sailing histories and memoirs. You've frugal but you spend more for things of quality, knowing they'll last longer. You're constantly on the lookout for a good deal or for freebies.

You've started to hoard items that could be useful for boat repairs, like scrap metal and engine parts. More of your time is spent looking for that block or fairlead you removed from one boat and want to install on another. The "shipshape" condition of your neighbours' boats inspires you to spend weekends scrubbing your deck, polishing your brightwork, power-washing and waxing the hull. You get a sense of satisfaction when everything is stowed away properly—sails folded and flaked, lines coiled. This tendency creeps into your home and other areas of your life. You embrace minimalism and the Marie Kondo method, and you consider downgrading from a three-bedroom house to a thousand-square-foot houseboat. Things are in a complete jumble before they are relentlessly tidy, vacillating between these two states.

You've always made an effort to be on time, though it's difficult in the city with its sirens and short turns and endless constructions and suturings of asphalt. You've always had a propensity to be running ten minutes behind, but since you've started filling your calendar with ferry and tender schedules, dinghy and keelboat classes, weeknight races, early-morning regattas, race committee duties, and volunteer work parties, you're more motivated to be punctual. Being late means having to catch the next ferry, missing class instruction, and causing an inconvenience to your skipper and crew. Worst of all, it means less time on the water. In fact, you start showing up early, because there's always something to do—minor repairs, the unglamorous job of pumping out, someone else you agreed to help.

You check the weather before leaving the house, pushing an umbrella into your knapsack. You pull out your sweaters as the leaves start to yellow and fade. You make plans for a picnic or to start the garden when the ground's no longer soft from melted snow. But now you also check storm warnings and wind directions on your PredictWind app. Now you watch the leaves fluttering, nature's ticklers that give a hint of how much breeze there will be on the lake. Now you can't walk down a street as gusts rattle windows and storefront signs without thinking about how, if you were sailing, you'd have to put a reef in and clamber to the high side. When you feel cool air on the side of your face, you know there's wind coming from the east. If there's a steady afternoon breeze and rain-clouds hovering over the glassy, indifferent condos, you can deduce that they'll likely be blown out of the city so the race can still take place that evening. Now the landscape is a topography of wind and you're better at reading its shifts and lulls.

You've begun unconsciously, then consciously, classifying people into two groups: Those You Would Trust on a Sailboat and Those Who Are Clearly More Comfortable on Land. Or, more simply: Sailors and Non-Sailors. In the first category are people who love being on, near, or in water and whose company you enjoy in close quarters for long periods of time. The second category of people, though no less valuable, are prone to motion sickness, less aware of their surroundings. You might also think twice about inviting out friends and family who can't abide authority, who can't keep a thought to themselves, or who are easily distracted by shiny objects.

Doubtless, there are sailors whose barking or patronizing company you can't stand, as well as non-sailors you would trust with your life. These are fluid categories, and you can occupy your mind with further complexities and subcategories, such as Sailors You Would Crew With and Sailors You Wouldn't, and so on. Increasingly, your social circle is made up of sailors, because there are certain things only other sailors can understand. These include the giddiness of being afloat

again after a long absence from the water, the anxiety of a
boat repair that keeps a mind awake until the small hours, and
the soft pleasure of replaying a recent cruise or race. There
are sides of yourself that emerge only when you're on a boat.
You're happier, more relaxed, and more focused. You don't
check your phone as much and you don't have that chaffed
feeling of wanting to be somewhere else.

If you're single, you try your utmost not to have romantic
feelings about another sailor, especially if you're both members of the same club. Flirtation is acceptable, but you look
away when they are hooking up a spinnaker or bending over
a winch in the cockpit. You are aware, with your sailor's sense
of observation, whenever they are in proximity, and you are
also aware of the club's penchant for gossip. You're protective
of this precious space where you can be yourself, show up
without makeup in your frayed clothes, and you would hate
for any awkwardness. If both of you succumb to your feelings and have a happily-ever-after ending, there is no choice
but to get married in the clubhouse.

You and your sailing life-partner plan your calendars around
racing and cruising. Your arguments are about whether to buy
a Beneteau or a C&C. Sailing together brings you closer now
that you have to define your roles: navigation, provisioning,
cleaning, cooking, and helming. No age is too young to get
your kids accustomed to being aboard, and before they can
even spell properly, your kid has gripped a tiller, has come
back from sailing camp full of new-found confidence after
righting a capsized Sunfish or Optimist on their own. If you
are going through a breakup or divorce, you are comforted
by the knowledge that you'll be spared the trouble of retelling the story because it'll spread throughout the club like an

invasive plant, self-seeding around picnic tables, finger docks, and lockers. If you're newly single and need to know if someone you're interested in is available, you can find out through the grapevine. It disturbs you, a private person, that so much is known about your personal life, but you're also resigned to it like an inescapable squall that you have to ride out.

You tried not to let sailing take over your identity. It started innocuously enough, by accepting an invitation to crew or signing up for a class, and before you knew it, the bug had bitten. You're now reading sailing manuals, watching YouTube videos about cruises around the Great Lakes or race tactics, and have downloaded audiobooks about solo ocean crossings. You cultivate other hobbies, such as life drawing, hockey, or dance classes, to seem like a well-rounded person at parties, so that you don't seem boring to non-sailing friends and family. You might not bring up sailing to new acquaintances, on first dates, or to colleagues, because once you get started on the topic, it's hard to shut you up. Some people have known you for decades without being aware that you sail. Maybe you don't want to seem privileged or pretentious. From time to time, you might post a photo on social media, unable to resist showing off. After all, you're proud of your skills. You collect more and more sailing stories and it's hard not to share them. The scenery is too beautiful to keep to yourself—views of golden sunsets, harbours pinned with taut, triangular sails, fog whispering along the shoreline.

Then there's the List. This is a list that you haven't revealed to anyone, maybe not even to yourself, of adventures still to come. Sailing all five of the Great Lakes. Sailing offshore. An overnight cruise. On online crewbanks, you read about opportunities to join a captain to sail around the Greek Islands.

Some are paid positions, some specify solo and nightwatches. Other skippers will pay for everyone on board; you only have to cover the cost of getting to where the boat is moored. The List might also include certain races and regattas, like a one-design race, a pursuit or fiasco race, a long-distance race. Maybe you have ambitions to compete in a championship, invitational, or international regatta. You daydream about flying to New England to race their Frostbite series or to the southern hemisphere, where regattas are held in winter months. Or you follow news of the Vendée Globe, a single-handed non-stop around-the-world race held every four years and considered to be the biggest challenge of a solo sailor's endurance and skills. Your ambitions might be more humble: simply finishing a race with a new crew or winning a club flag in a weeknight race series.

When you go camping, your friends are impressed by your knot-tying abilities.

You find yourself repeating instructions back at people, just to ensure they know you heard them.

On rocking buses and subways, you can balance without holding on to anything.

Your colleagues praise your calmness when your workplace is chaotic with urgent deadlines, unhappy clients, and miscommunications.

You might be prone to exaggeration and telling long stories.

When someone says how well things are going, you can't help but knock on wood.

You swallow your pride and ask for help after struggling all day with a repair.

You've always considered yourself observant, but your attention used to be scattered. You noticed details in a fleeting, jumbled way, like a crumb on your sleeve, the crinkle around a friend's eyes as they catch your gaze, the light as it tosses itself around your kitchen. Before, your attention was underutilized at close range. Spending season after season scoping out perimeters, watching the current and looking for dark patches on the water, gazing ahead at the racecourse marks or at how other boats are trimming their sails, has made your attention more expansive. Wherever you are, you scan your surroundings. You note, from across the atrium, a familiar face. On a dark street, you can sense from the corner of your eye a young woman crossing the road, a stranger getting into their car, a food delivery biker pedalling up the hill. With your powers of observation, you are constantly planning your next move. You don't miss much. You might pretend not to have noticed someone or something, but that is only camouflage. Having spent hours squinting at the shape of a sail, attuned to its luffs and flutters, you've gained the ability to hyperfocus. And if you miss something, don't worry. Another sailor will point it out, along with your lapse.

Dear Wayfarer

WE HAVEN'T MET YET but I've seen your picture. In ads from Parry Sound, Montreal, and Michigan, your wide hull sits on a tilting trailer, your mast rests lengthwise across your wooden deck. I want to unlatch the stern bulkhead storage that Wayfarers are famous for, run my hands over your wooden bench seats. I squint, trying to ascertain if your owner has taken good care of you, has rubbed you with varnish and kept you indoors out of snowdrifts. I call and email your owners, hoping they can tell me something about you that will make this decision feel watertight. One changes his mind about selling you, another tells me about multiple bidders, and one more has recently become a widower and isn't ready to sell you yet.

Until a month ago I had no idea Wayfarers existed. I always knew I would own a boat someday, but it occurred to me last fall that the sooner I do, the most use I'll get out of it. I'm tired of waiting for invitations from other people to go sailing. I've learned to become a competent crew member, and now it's time to take the helm myself, to choose my own course.

I'm attracted to lean and mean racing boats—Sharks, J24s, Vikings—but buying a bigger keelboat means having to race against my former skippers, having to train and retain a crew, and paying for senior membership and mooring fees. I'm not ready yet. A dinghy is the other option, a vessel I could rig and sail on my own. There are plenty of used and new options available: an Ideal 18, a Laser, or an Albacore, or even the plastic-hulled RS Quests I learned to sail on. They're common around Lake Ontario, but these fibreglass and polycarbonate boats have no character for me. If I'm going to own a boat, why not own something beautiful?

You came up in a Google search as one of the most stable dinghies. I don't like capsizing—who does? I admire sailors who aren't fazed by it, but I don't want to sail a tippy boat or one that requires me to be hiked out and harnessed like an aerial gymnast. You're known as the cruising dinghy, and I've heard stories of ocean voyages, seen owners sew canvas tents that hang over the boom to create a cozy, waterproof space for sleeping. That's when I began to dream of overnight cruising trips around the Great Lakes, pulling you onto a sandy shore using fenders as rollers, and sleeping bathed in silence.

New Wayfarers, made of fibreglass and hand-built by Hartley Boats in the UK, cost nearly $20,000 Canadian. You only cost three grand, though I know there will be other expenses. I'll need a boat survey and insurance, and to rent a car to transport you to the islands. I'll need an electric motor, oars, and spare parts I don't know the name of yet. I've heard BOAT is an acronym for "break out another thousand." My dad shares this view. He still urges me to save for a down payment, but surely there is room in my life to be fanciful and spontaneous. I've always been careful and prudent, never done anything without thorough research, but I don't want to become paralyzed by indecision.

Am I going through a mid-life crisis? I don't expect you to know the answer—you're a sixteen-foot boat, not a therapist. Well, technically you're fifteen feet and ten inches long, six feet across your hull. I've read your specifications sheet, that you displace 370 pounds, that you were designed by Ian Proctor and first went into production in 1957. Over ten thousand Wayfarers exist in the world. I'm five foot three-and-a -half inches tall, I weigh around 150 pounds depending on the time of year, I was born in 1981, and there are a hundred million people with the surname Wang. I was designed by two nonconforming Chinese artist hippie parents who emigrated to Canada in 1970. I don't have children, I'm not married, and I still rent my home. I don't own anything more expensive than a second-hand bike and a laptop. I want to own things that don't take up much space and that have a story.

I worry that I'm not the best person to care for you. I met another Wayfarer owner and boat builder. Kit has carpentry skills, a garage that protects his rebuilt *Peregrine* from the Toronto damp, and races at the Toronto Sailing & Canoe Club with other Wayfarer owners. As he was showing me his beautifully maintained boat, I felt doubt in his gaze, though I might have imagined it. Countless people have told me that fibreglass boats are easier to maintain, and I admit I have my qualms about whether I can care for you properly. I thought I knew a lot about sailing, but owning a wooden boat is a new world of rigging, maintenance, epoxy, and varnish.

I've been ordering books, reading assembly manuals, forums, and Facebook group posts, feeling overwhelmed but also excited. I'm not deterred by thoughts of repairing, sanding, painting, and varnishing. To be honest, it sounds kind of fun, a refreshing change from my screencentric life-style. And if it gets to be too much for me, I'll ask for help. I've always been proud to be self-reliant, but as I get older, I'm more comfortable with the idea of depending on others. I have learned from crewing that my fierce sense of indepen-dence is not compromised by having helping hands. Sailors are so ready to give advice that I would surely be depriving them of a great sense satisfaction if I insisted on doing every-thing myself.

And you're part of a beautiful community, Wayfarer. I understand that boat owners need others to complain to, to ask advice of, to share adventures with. I've heard about the annual Wayfarer cruising rallies to Maine or the Thousand Islands or Georgian Bay. It restores my faith that such gather-ings take place between strangers who love sailing the same type of boat, that a gesture to claim my independence will, in fact, still connect me with others. There's a long list of people I could learn from and who could learn with me. Amanda, Mark, Phil, Quentin, Tala, and Jade, everyone at the club I've crewed with, new members and friends, fellow writers and editors, co-workers and comrades. But I also hope we'll have many hours alone together, once I'm confident enough to helm under Lake Ontario's gusty winds. I'm looking forward to stowing a cot, tent, and sleeping bag under your foredeck, my blue enamel camping set in your stern bulkhead, supplies in a dry sail bag, tied down with bungee cords. I'm planning on so many adventures together.

Wayfarer, my ancestors were not all good people. I don't know why I'm telling you this. One of my grandfathers owned factories and likely had little concern for his workers.

My other grandfather spent more on whisky than he did on his children, but he could also do calligraphy and make lanterns. My grandmothers beat their kids and neglected them, and as a result, my parents carry trauma in their bones. I'm still proud of what they gave me—a love of art and beautiful things, lifetimes of stories and conversation. My mother tells me that in my Chinese Four Pillars horoscope, I have an imbalance of elements, and I'm in need of water and wood. The more time I spend on or in water, or in forested groves, around books and paper, the better. She understands that my craving for you comes from a need in my body to right a balance.

And is there a better way to find balance than in a dinghy? Where not having enough ballast or not quickly ducking the boom after a tack would mean plunging into cold lake water? I get nervous thinking about the breakages and disasters that might happen out in the middle of a lake, miles from shore. I'll need to run a righting line outside the hull, get my Pleasure Craft Operator Card, buy a handheld GPS, flares, an air horn, towing lines. What if, as we're sailing around the Leslie Street Spit, the current pushes us against the rocks? What if I see flashes of lightning in the distance and have a panic attack? I wish you could write back to me and tell me how to avoid accumulating phobias and how to prepare.

If you and I end up together, I'm in this for the long haul. I'm not the type of person who will buy a boat every year. I'm not even the type of person who upgrades their phone every year. I still use an iPhone 7. I have five pairs of the same type of jeans, each in a different colour. I've recently patched up two of them. I hold on to things. I hope to be a Wayfarer sailor until I'm too old to push your dolly down the dinghy ramp. Then I plan to donate you to the club so that future generations can feel what it's like to sail a wooden craft. You're a piece of history, and wooden boats are in danger of vanishing. Queen City used to be all wooden boats. You and I will be going against the trend, but I've never been one of those cool kids who picks the latest, popular models. I'm anachronistic and bookish. If you take care of me, I'll take care of you. Just kidding—even if you cut and bruise me, I'll still take care of you. I'm accustomed to mild forms of abuse and punishment. That's just my sense of humour. You'll have to get used to it.

Wayfarer, I've been practising my knots. I can attach your sails with bowlines, and stop lines from running out of fairleads and blocks with a figure eight. I'll tie your fenders on with clove hitches. I'm tied to my family with sheet bends, and they're braided to the land. Our houses are tied to us with slipknots, ready to be pulled loose. Our responsibilities tighten like constrictor knots but can slide and move down the line. Humans are bound to so many things that I wonder if we're ever truly free. Our freedoms have limited range. Our freedoms are bound by our bodies, always needing more water and oxygen and iron pumping into our blood. Our bodies aren't seaworthy like you. And you are in need of hands. You're in need of someone to carry. When we meet under the budding trees next spring, we'll see what else ties us together.

With love,
Phoebe

Notes

RELATIVE TO WIND is not meant to tell every sailor's story, and instead is a recounting of my personal experience and learning process. As a result, my views of other individuals and communities is limited. In some cases, I have respected the privacy of individuals who have asked not to be identified or for stories not to be shared. Even having taken these precautions, it is still possible that I have infringed upon others' stories or made errors regarding the events in this book, and for that I apologize and welcome feedback.

Sailing is a highly technical sport, and it also can proliferate many different interpretations and perspectives. This results in differing opinions and conflicting information. The learning process is one that takes years, and as a result, I am still adding to my understanding of sailing. I hope that all sailors, those who have yet to sail, and lifelong learners, will find something of themselves here.

BECOMING CREW: The majority of these essays are located at Queen City Yacht Club, one of the numerous yacht clubs in the Lake Ontario region. It is on the Toronto Island, a fifteen-minute ferry ride from downtown Toronto, Ontario, Canada. More about the club can be found at qcyc.ca.

BOAT WORDS: I reference the excellent compilation of nautical terminology and history, Robert McKenna's *Dictionary of Nautical Literacy* (International Marine / McGraw Hill, 2001).

FREE BEER: Mark Macrae is an actor and musician originally from Fredericton, New Brunswick, and now residing in Toronto, Ontario, with whom I began crewing in 2008. His website can be found here: markmacrae.ca. His Wordpress sailing blog is here: n26panache.wordpress.com.

I refer to Sail Canada's *2021–2024 Racing Rules of Sailing* with Sail Canada Prescriptions published in 2020 and which can be ordered through Sail Canada or your local nautical bookstore. Performance Handicap Racing Fleet for Lake Ontario (PHRF-LO) manuals can be found here: phrf-lo.org.

According to the Ontario Liquor Licence Act, it is prohibited to consume alcohol on a sailboat or motorboat while it is in motion, and passengers can only drink alcohol if the boat has cooking, sleeping, and toilet facilities and is moored to a dock, beached, or at anchor. This book represents instances of alcohol consumption that are illustrative of sailing and yacht club culture but does not condone excessive and unsafe drinking while under sail. If you do choose to consume alcohol on a boat, please do so safely, keep your consumption under the legal limit, and remember that even a small amount of alcohol can increase the risk of accidents on board.

The word *handicap*, when defined as a physical or mental difficulty, is an outdated and ablest term that labels people with disabilities negatively. In the context of this book, I have used *handicap* to refer to a disadvantage imposed on a superior competitor in sports such as golf, horse racing, and competitive sailing in order to make the chances more equal, as defined by the *Canadian Oxford Dictionary*. I have kept this word in my book because Performance Handicap Racing Fleet organization is a proper name and "handicap ratings" is a commonly used term in sailing, but I call on sports and sailing communities and organizations to consider language that is more inclusive and respectful of people with disabilities. Language matters.

RELATIVE TO WIND: My very first manual on sailing was a second-hand copy of Rob MacLeod's *Basic Sailing and Cruising Skills* written for the Canadian Yachting Association and first published in 1985. I have pored over its pages so often and through so many long winters, and I have rarely found clearer drawings or more straightforward explanations elsewhere. It can be read online in full on the Internet Archive.

Dallas Murphy's *Plain Sailing: Learning to See Like a Sailor: A Manual of Sail Trim* (Burford Books, 2010) is an excellent book on getting started in sailing and sail trim.

KNOWING WHEN TO QUIT: The Lake Ontario Racing Circuit is an association of sailing clubs in the Greater Toronto Area whose members organize and promote competitive keelboat sailing in the GTA, including a Racing Circuit Series. Visit lorc.org to learn more.

Lake Ontario Offshore Racing: loor.ca

Lake Yacht Racing Association: lyrawaters.org

AHMEN: ahmen.ca

BECALMED: Publications and websites that I consulted for this essay include Environment Canada, National Geographic Society's Education website, NASA Earth Observatory, the Online Etymology Dictionary, Poetry Foundation, the National Gallery (London), National Gallery of Art, National Maritime Museum (Greenwich), Royal Museums Greenwich, the *Washington Post*, and the Museum of Fine Arts Boston.

For further reading on the topic of maritime art, George S. Keyes's *Mirror of Empire: Dutch Marine Art of Seventeenth Century* (Minneapolis Institute of Arts, 1990) and Christine Riding et al.'s *Turner & the Sea* (Thames & Hudson Ltd., 2013) are excellent texts.

David Dabydeen's views on Turner have been discussed in Sarah Fulford's article "David Dabydeen and Turner's Sublime Aesthetic," published in *Anthurium: A Caribbean Studies Journal*, Volume 3, Issue 1, June 2005.

THE BADLANDS: More about the eastern cottonwood can be found through the Government of Canada's Canadian Forest Service and the Government of Ontario's Environment and Energy Tree Atlas.

Graham Day's *Community and Everyday Life* (Routledge, 2006) provided me with a crash course on the sociological and community theories of Ferdinand Tönnies, Émile Durkheim, Max Weber, and Talcott Parsons. Raymond Williams's essay "The Importance of Community" can be found in *Resources of Hope: Culture, Democracy, Socialism* (Verso, 1989).

BURIED TIMBER: I relied heavily on Nathan Ng's Historical Maps of Toronto website, for which he has compiled a free and accessible list of maps by date from Library and Archives

Canada, City of Toronto Archives, and other sources.

The Toronto Historical Association's list of lost sites and the Toronto Public Library digital archives, the Queen City archives organized by Richard Slee, and Wayne Lilley's centennial publication, *Queen City Yacht Club 1889–1989*, were also invaluable sources of the club's history.

CONTROLLED CAPSIZE: The CANSail Program is Sail Canada's national learn-to-sail program, recognized by World Sailing and taught by certified instructors. Numerous clubs in Canada offer CANSail classes, and more information can be found here: sailing.ca / cansail.

THE SUMMER OF ENDLESS FUN, PART 2: Queen City Yacht Club has a new YouTube channel for historical films that can be viewed here: youtube.com / @qcychistory4418.

The Canadian Asian Sailors is a community group based in Toronto supporting Canadian Asian sailors! The Instagram account is @canadian_asian_sailors.

IN PURSUIT: This essay follows the format of typical sailing race or regatta sailing instructions, which are required documents for any event that complies with the Racing Rules of Sailing. They are meant to express the intentions of the race committee, technical committee, and protest committee, and the obligations of competitors, but I have taken a great deal of poetic licence with the contents.

Acknowledgements

I LIVE AND WORK on the traditional territory of many nations, including the Mississaugas of the Credit, the Anishinaabeg, the Chippewa, the Haudenosaunee, and the Huron Wendat peoples, who have cared for the lands and waters of Lake Ontario and its surroundings for many millennia. The City of Toronto is now also home to many First Nations, Inuit, and Métis peoples.

Thank you, Mark Macrae, who invited me out for a sail one September evening in 2009 and who has supported this project with his time, knowledge, and stories. Much love to all of *Panache*'s crew: Pat, Amanda, Quentin, Phil, Tim, Jade, Tala, and all of the many friendly faces that have joined us over the years. I'm grateful to those skippers who welcomed me aboard so generously: Eric Whan, Ron Mazza, Bruce Smith, Neale Martin, Rob Mew, and Roel Vanderwal. Thank you to Jess Mace, Graham Dougal, and Richard Slee, who gave their time to this project, and to the members of Queen City Yacht Club, who make it such a special place; you are too many to name but I see all of you. I'm grateful for the welcome I received from the Kingston Yacht Club. Thank you to Amanda Song and Jianpeng Wang for creating the sailing community I had always been looking for.

My immense gratitude to my editor Andrew Faulkner and publisher Leigh Nash for seeing that this book was in me and believing in this manuscript so passionately. Assembly Press is a gift to writers and readers. Thank you to the multi-talented poet and editor Stuart Ross for proofreading, and to Greg Tabor for the wonderful cover and interior design. I also wish to thank Souvankham Thammavongsa for passing on "Boat Words" to the editors at *Brick* magazine, who published an earlier version of this essay, and to Zak Jones for inviting me to give a talk at Trampoline Hall, where I delivered an early draft of "Relative to Wind."

Thanks to my parents, who inspired me with their adventurous natures.

This book is dedicated to sailors everywhere, including sailors to be.

PHOTO CREDIT: LUCY LU

PHOEBE WANG is a writer, educator, and sailor based in Toronto, Canada, and a first-generation Chinese Canadian from the traditional and unceded territory of the Anishinaabe Algonquin in Ottawa. Her first collection of poetry, *Admission Requirements* (McClelland & Stewart, 2017), was shortlisted for the Gerald Lambert Memorial Award, the Pat Lowther Memorial Award, and nominated for the Trillium Book Award, and her second collection is *Waking Occupations* (McClelland & Stewart, 2022). She served as Writer-in-Residence at the University of New Brunswick in 2021–2022. She is a poetry editor with Brick Books, a mentor in the MA in Creative Writing program at the University of Toronto, and works as a Writing and Learning Consultant for ELL students at OCAD University. More of her work can be found at alittleprint.com.